EU Procedural Rights in Criminal Proceedings

D1728202

European Commission   Directorate General
Justice and Home Affairs

Justice Freedom and Security

EU Procedural Rights in Criminal Proceedings

Taru Spronken
Gert Vermeulen
Dorris de Vocht
Laurens van Puyenbroeck

Maklu

Antwerp | Apeldoorn | Portland

T. Spronken, G. Vermeulen, D. de Vocht en L. van Puyenbroeck
EU Procedural Rights in Criminal Proceedings
Antwerp – Apeldoorn – Portland
Maklu
2009

116 p. - 16 x 24cm
ISBN 978-90-466-0317-8
D/2009/1997/74
NUR 824

Maklu-Publishers
Somersstraat 13/15, 2018 Antwerpen, Belgium, info@maklu.be
Koninginnenlaan 96, 7315 EB Apeldoorn, The Netherlands, info@maklu.be
www. maklu.eu

USA & Canada
International Specialized Book Services
920 NE 58th Ave, Suite 300, Portland, OR 97213-3786, orders@isbs.com
www.isbs.com

UK & Ireland
R. Bayliss, 81 Milehouse Road, Plymouth, Devon PL3 4AE

Contact Details

This research was carried out by prof. dr. Taru Spronken (project coordinator) and dr. Dorris de Vocht (Faculty of Law, Department of Criminal law and Criminology, Maastricht University) together with prof. dr. Gert Vermeulen and Laurens van Puyenbroeck (Institute for International Research on Criminal Policy, Ghent University). The research has been funded by the European Commission. The views expressed in this publication cannot be taken to represent the official opinion of the European Commission.

Contact details for the University of Maastricht:

 **Maastricht University**

Prof. Dr. Taru Spronken
Professor of Criminal Law, Faculty of Law, Department of Criminal Law and Criminology
University of Maastricht
P.O. Box 616
6200 MD Maastricht
The Netherlands
Tel: +31 43 388 27 78
Email: taru.spronken@maastrichtuniversity.nl

Dr. Dorris de Vocht
Assistant professor, Faculty of Law, Department of Criminal Law and Criminology
University of Maastricht
P.O. Box 616
6200 MD Maastricht
The Netherlands
Tel: +31 43 38 33 99
Email: dorris.devocht@maastrichtuniversity.nl

Contact details for Ghent University:

Institute for International Research on Criminal Policy
Ghent University

Prof. Dr. Gert Vermeulen
Professor of Criminal Law, Faculty of Law, Department of Criminal Law and
Criminology
Ghent University
Universiteitsstraat 4
9000 Gent
Belgium
Tel: +32 9 264 69 43
Fax: + 32 9 264 84 94
Email: Gert.Vermeulen@UGent.be

Laurens van Puyenbroeck
Academic Assistant, Faculty of Law, Department of Criminal Law and
Criminology
Ghent University
Universiteitsstraat 4
9000 Gent
Belgium
Tel: +32 9 264 97 02
Fax: + 32 9 264 69 71
Email: Laurens.vanPuyenbroeck@UGent.be

Technical design, implementation and support of online questionnaire:

Jasper Holthuis and Guido Athmer, PrimaID Maastricht
the Netherlands
www.primaid.nl

Contact details for the European Commission DG Justice and Home Affairs:

European Commission
DG Justice& Home Affairs
Caroline Morgan
Unit D3 – Criminal Justice
DG Justice and Home Affairs
European Commission
B-1049 Brussels
Belgium
Tel: +32 2 296 0067
Fax: +32 2 296 7634
Email: caroline.morgan@cec.eu.int

This report and the annexes 1, 2 and 3 with the complete research data will be available online: http://arno.unimaas.nl/show.cgi?fid=16315

The report was finalised on 8 September 2009

Table of contents

List of Abbreviations:

CPT	The European Committee for the Prevention of Torture and Inhuman or Degrading Treatment or Punishment
EC	European Commission
ECHR	European Convention on Human Rights
ECtHR	European Court of Human Rights
ECmHR	European Commission of Human Rights
EU	European Union
Green Paper	Green Paper from the Commission on Procedural Safeguards for Suspects and Defendants in Criminal Proceedings throughout the European Union 19 February 2003, COM (2003) 75 final
ICCPR	International Convention on Civil and Political Rights
Proposed FD	Proposal for a Council Framework Decision on certain procedural rights in criminal proceedings throughout the European Union, 28 April 2004, COM (2004) 328 final, 2004/0113 (CNS)

Executive Summary

Procedural rights in criminal proceedings have received an increasing amount of attention in the European Union over the last couple of years and are the central topic of this research project.

All EU Member States are party to the European Convention on Human Rights, which is the principal treaty setting out the basic standards for suspects' procedural rights in criminal proceedings in the EU. However, divergent practices in different Member States have hitherto hindered mutual trust and confidence, principles put forward by the 1999 Tampere Conclusions[1], between them. In order to counter this obstacle identified by the European Commission in its 2003 Green Paper on "Procedural Safeguards for Suspects and Defendants in Criminal Proceedings throughout the EU"[2], the Commission held that the EU is justified in taking action in this field. Member States had also expressed the need and wish for cooperation in the matter on a European level. However, the ideas in the 2004 "Proposal for a Council Framework Decision on certain procedural rights in criminal proceedings throughout the European Union" have not yet sparked any political agreement on the matter.

In 2005, the Commission arranged for a study to be carried out on procedural rights in the EU, in order to comply with the The Hague Programme's call for studies on the existing levels of safeguards in the Member States.[3]

This study has been carried out as a follow-up report to the 2005 study to obtain up to date information on the level of provision of procedural rights in the Member States that can provide a lead for a possible new Commission legal initiative on the matter.

---

[1] See G. Vernimmen-Van Tiggelen and Laura Surano, Analysis of the future of mutual recognition in criminal matters in the European Union, 20 November 2008.
[2] Green Paper from the Commission 'Procedural Safeguards for Suspects and Defendants in Criminal Proceedings throughout the European Union', Brussels, 19 February 2003, COM (2003) 75 final.
[3] T.N.B.M. Spronken and M. Attinger, Procedural Rights in criminal proceedings: Existing Level of Safeguards in the European Union, funded and published by the European Commission, 12 December 2005 <http://arno.unimaas.nl/show.cgi?fid=3891>

The report aims at providing an overview of the *status quo* of 4 fundamental procedural rights in criminal proceedings in the EU Member States:

- The right to information,
- The right to legal advice,
- The right to legal assistance free of charge,
- The right to translation and interpretation of documents

First, an analysis is offered of these procedural rights which the European Convention on Human Rights provides for, as dealt with in recent case law of the European Court of Human Rights. Secondly, the report paints a picture of the extent to which these procedural rights are guaranteed in the formal legislation of each EU Member State. This overview was obtained through an extensive questionnaire[4] which was sent out to all 27 EU Member States. The questionnaire also included questions on how the examined procedural rights are dealt with in the Member States within procedures concerning the European Arrest Warrant (EAW) and other mutual recognition instruments. The right to information was dealt with in the questionnaire as an overarching horizontal issue and not as a separate right, as is the case for the analysis of the European Court of Human Rights-case law. Therefore, the questionnaire was divided into the following chapters:

Chapter 1:   The right to legal advice
Chapter 2:   The right to legal assistance (partially) free of charge
Chapter 3:   The right to translation of documents and the right to interpretation
Chapter 4:   Other fundamental guarantees and the right to be informed on them
Chapter 5:   European Arrest Warrant and other mutual recognition instruments

---

[4] See annex 1

The conclusions drawn in the study are based on the answers as provided for by the representatives of the Ministries of Justice of the Member States. It is important to note that the project team has not carried out any research on the accuracy of these answers. All Member States replied to the questionnaire except for Malta, so the conclusions are based on the information given by 26 Member States.

The following conclusions were reached:

The right to information

In this study, the right to information is dealt with as an overarching horizontal issue that is highly relevant for procedural rights being practical and effective. We have distinguished 2 dimensions. First, the right of anyone charged with a criminal offence to be informed on the nature and cause of the accusations against him and to have access to the evidence on which these accusations are based as guaranteed by Art. 5 and 6 ECHR. Secondly, the right to information in the sense of being informed on fundamental procedural rights, which as such is not covered by the ECHR.

A notable finding of this study is the fact that the right to remain silent is no statutory right in France and Luxembourg and the right to have access to the file is not provided for on behalf of the suspect in legislation in Estonia, France, Germany and Spain, both being basic requirements of a fair trial in the ECHR.

A remark applicable to all the rights that are object of this study (including the right to be informed on the charge) is the substantial divergence in the way suspects are informed as well as the absence of legal obligations for the authorities to inform the suspect on these fundamental procedural rights.

With regard to the right to contact a lawyer after arrest, all Member States have a legal obligation to inform the suspect on this right, but this information is not always given immediately after arrest. Also, the moment at which the obligation exists to inform the suspect of his right to have a lawyer present during police interrogation varies from promptly after arrest until a later stage in the investigation or proceedings. This right is obviously only effective when the suspect is timely informed on it and if he is offered the opportunity to contact a lawyer before the first police interrogation. In many Member States where there is a right to legal assistance during police interrogation, there are no provisions to secure the effectuation of this right.

The same applies to information on the right to legal aid. In 4 Member States there is no legal obligation to inform the suspect of the right to legal assistance (partially) free of charge and in the remainder of the Member States where a legal obligation to inform the suspect does exist, the moment at which the duty arises varies considerably as well as the manner in which the information is given. In the majority of the countries the information is given orally and in only 4 countries this information is provided in a letter of rights.

A similar picture can be drawn with regard to information on the right to interpretation and translation. In 8 Member States there is no legal obligation to inform the suspect on his right to interpretation and in 9 Member States there is no obligation to inform the suspect on his right to translation.

Striking is that in Belgium and Finland there is no legal obligation to inform the suspect of his right to silence and in 6 Member States there is no obligation to inform the suspect of his right to call and examine witnesses.

In 10 Member States the suspect is informed about (one or more of) his rights by means of a letter of rights (Austria, Czech Republic, England and Wales, Italy, Latvia, Luxemburg, Poland, Slovak Republic , Spain and Sweden). However, there are great differences between these EU Member States as to which rights are included. Many letters of rights do not mention the right to silence or the right to translation or interpretation and sometimes there is no letter of rights available in the language the suspect understands.

The right to legal assistance

According to the case law of the ECtHR the right to contact a legal advisor – as part of the general right to legal assistance which is covered by Art. 6 § 3 b and c ECHR – arises immediately upon arrest. The study shows that the right to contact a lawyer after arrest exists in most Member States. However, there is a great divergence as to the moment at which the right to contact a lawyer can be effected. For example, in a considerable number of countries this is not possible immediately after arrest – as required by the ECHR – but only at a given stage of the investigation or the proceedings.

Also, it follows from recent judgments of the ECtHR that access to a lawyer should as a rule be provided as from the first interrogation of a suspect by the police, unless it is demonstrated in the light of the particular circumstances of the case that there are compelling reasons to restrict this right. Furthermore, the ECtHR has held that the lack of legal assistance during a suspect's interrogation would constitute a restriction of his defence rights and that these rights will in principle be irretrievably prejudiced when incriminating statements, made during police interrogation without access to a lawyer, are used for a conviction.

It can be concluded from the study that the basic rules mentioned above are not common practice throughout the EU: in 4 Member States the right to consult a lawyer before questioning is not guaranteed[5] and in 5 Member States there is no right for the lawyer to be present at interrogations carried out by the police. In almost all countries where the lawyer is allowed to be present, authorities are obliged to inform the suspect of this right but there are considerable differences among Member States as to the moment at which the obligation to inform the suspect of this right arises and the way in which the information is provided to the suspect. Furthermore, in several countries there is no possibility for the defence to deliberate in private during questioning. Finally, the study shows that the presence of a lawyer at the interrogation is not deemed indispensable; only in 3 Member States it is not allowed using the confession of a suspect made in the absence of his lawyer as evidence in court.

The right to legal assistance (partially) free of charge

With respect to the right to legal assistance (partially) free of charge – as guaranteed by Art. 6 § 3 c ECHR – it follows from the case law of the ECtHR that Member States have a certain margin of appreciation in choosing a system that appears to them to be most effective. However, free legal assistance should always be available where the interests of justice demand it. The study shows that although the right to legal assistance (partially) free of charge exists in all Member States (with the exception of one) there are considerable differences in the implementation of this right. Especially striking is the wide variety in merits and/or means tests. Also important is the fact that in a small number of countries there is no legal obligation to inform the suspect of his right to legal assistance (partially) free of charge. Where this obligation does exist, there is considerable variation as to the scope of this obligation. Besides the differences in the

---

[5] In the Netherlands this has changed as a result of the Salduz judgment of the ECtHR Grand Chamber, 27 November 2008, *Salduz* (no. 36391/02). Requested to give an interpretation of the consequences of this judgment for the Dutch practice the Supreme Court of the Netherlands ruled on 30 June 2009 that a suspect has the right to consult a lawyer before the first police interrogation, but that only a juvenile suspect has the right to also have a lawyer present during police interrogation (HR 30 June 2009, no. 2411.08 J, NbSr 2009, 249.

applicable legal frameworks regulating the right to legal assistance free of charge, the study also shows enormous differences in financial recourses available for legal aid. The remarkable low budgets of some countries raise the question whether despite existing guarantees in the applicable legal framework, it is– in everyday practice – in fact possible to effectuate the right to free legal assistance whenever the interest of justice demands it.

Quality of legal assistance (partially) free of charge

The study allows making some remarks as to the quality of the legal assistance (partially) free of charge and the responsibilities of the State in this respect. Although it is clear from the case law of the ECtHR that the lawyer's conduct is essentially an affair between the lawyer and his client, the State is under the obligation to ensure that legal assistance is effective. As a result, the Member States need to provide for some sort of monitoring system. The study shows that in a considerable number of countries there are no mechanisms to control the quality of legal assistance free of charge and in other Member States the authorities carrying out this kind of control vary widely. Consequently, there seems to be a substantial divergence in the way the quality of free legal assistance is controlled and ensured. Also, the 'special' requirements for the lawyer providing legal assistance free of charge are, in many cases, of a rather general nature and not limited to providing legal assistance free of charge. Moreover, in the majority of countries the specialisation and the availability of the lawyer are not taken into account when deciding on which lawyer to appoint to a case.

These findings raise the question on whether or not the quality of legal assistance (partially) free of charge is in fact sufficiently guaranteed throughout the EU.

The right to interpretation and translation

Although the right to interpretation exists in all Member States, the right to translation of documents is guaranteed in all but 5 Member States. The analysis shows a great divergence regarding the implementation of these rights. This divergence specifically applies to whether there is a legal obligation to be informed on these rights and to the scope of the rights. In 5 Member States there is no provision for interpretation at the consultation of the suspect with his lawyer and some Member States have no provisions for suspects who are visually impaired or hearing impaired. There is also a considerable variety as to which documents have to be provided to the suspect, and what documents are translated. It appears from the study that only a slight majority of the Member States provides a written translation of the charge, the detention order, or the final judgment. A letter of rights is only translated in 4 of the 10 countries that provide for one. The results of the study show that on the level of practical implementation of the right to interpretation and translation there is a divergence with the requirements that derive from the case law of the ECtHR as summarised in § 2.4.

Procedural rights in the mutual recognition instruments

When comparing the results of the analysis between the various mutual recognition instruments, some main findings can be distinguished quite easily. Firstly, the European Arrest Warrant (EAW) clearly is the instrument that is treated the most as being equal to the domestic proceedings. The right to legal advice, for example, is applied to EAW proceedings in all Member States in the same way as for domestic cases. Secondly, conclusions as to the 'partial' application of certain rights in regard of mutual recognition instruments should be made with caution since some Member States have responded in this way whereas the particular instrument has not yet been implemented into national law. Thirdly, those Member States not applying certain rights with regards to the various mutual recognition instruments are often the same. Finally, the great majority of Member States apply the right to information on fundamental procedural guarantees to the mutual recognition proceedings equally as for domestic proceedings.

Overall conclusion

A striking finding is the fact that fundamental rights such as the right to remain silent, to have access to the file and to call and/or examine witnesses or experts, which are basic requirements of a fair trial in the ECHR, are not provided for in the legislation of all Member States.

In general, it follows from the study that although the 4 procedural rights that were the subject of this research – the right to information, the right to legal advice, the right to legal assistance (partially) free of charge and the right to interpretation and translation – seem to be guaranteed by law more or less in accordance with the ECHR in the criminal justice systems of the EU. However, a more in depth look at the implementation of these rights raises doubts as to whether in all Member States everyday practice is in line with the Strasbourg standard. This underlines the need for EU action.

1   Introduction

1.1   Background

Even though all EU Member States are party to the ECHR (the principal treaty setting out the basic standards for suspects' procedural rights in the EU), divergent practices have hitherto hindered mutual trust and confidence, the principles put forward by the 1999 Tampere Conclusions.[6] In order to counter this obstacle identified by the European Commission in its 2003 Green Paper on "Procedural Safeguards for Suspects and Defendants in Criminal Proceedings throughout the EU"[7], the Commission held that the EU is justified in taking action in this field. Indeed, higher visibility and transparency would improve understanding on the part of all actors in the criminal justice systems in the Member States. The ideas in the 2004 "Proposal for a Council Framework Decision on certain procedural rights in criminal proceedings throughout the European Union"[8] (further referred to as 'the 2004 proposal'), where reiterated in the The Hague Programme, which states that "the further realisation of mutual recognition as the cornerstone of judicial cooperation implies the development of equivalent standards for procedural rights in criminal proceeding, based on the studies of the existing level of safeguards in Member States and with due respect for their legal traditions".

The assessment of the levels of provisions of procedural rights at the time afforded to suspected persons in criminal proceedings throughout the EU, became subject of a study carried out by Taru Spronken and Marelle Attinger. The Final Report in this study analysing the data gathered by the European Commission through a questionnaire sent to the Ministries of Justice and Home Affairs in the Member States, was delivered on 12 December 2005.[9]

The 2004 Proposal did not aim to create new rights or to monitor compliance with those rights that already exist under the ECHR or other international or European instruments, but rather aimed at ensuring a reasonable level of

---

[6] See G. Vernimmen-Van Tiggelen and Laura Surano, Analysis of the future of mutual recognition in criminal matters in the European Union, 20 November 2008.

[7] Green Paper from the Commission 'Procedural Safeguards for Suspects and Defendants in Criminal.
Proceedings throughout the European Union', Brussels, 19 February 2003, COM (2003) 75 final.

[8] Proposal for a 'Council Framework Decision on certain Procedural rights in Criminal Proceedings throughout the European Union', Brussels, 28 April 2004, COM (2004) 328 final, 2004/0113 (CNS).

[9] T.N.B.M. Spronken and M. Attinger, Procedural Rights in criminal proceedings: Existing Level of Safeguards in the European Union, funded and published by the European Commission, 12 December 2005 http://arno.unimaas.nl/show.cgi?fid=3891.

protection for suspects and defendants in criminal proceedings (such as the introduction of a letter of rights) in order to comply with the principle of mutual recognition. Nevertheless no political agreement has been reached on the matter, *inter alia* because of the argument of some Member States that the ECHR adequately protects the rights of suspects and accused persons in the EU.

In light of the provisions in the Lisbon Treaty and taking into account the expressed disappointment of Member States towards the Commission, a follow up research to the 2005 Study has been carried out to obtain up-to-date information on the level of provision of procedural rights in the Member States that can provide a lead for a possible new Commission legal initiative on the matter. The research can also provide inspiration for the current and future legislative work on several procedural rights, as envisaged in the Roadmap on Procedural Rights presented by the Swedish Presidency on 1 July 2009 (11457/09, DROIPEN 53, COPEN 120), in particular on the right to interpretation and translation as addressed in the proposed Framework Decision on the matter (see COM (2009) 338 final).

1.2   Methodology and structure

The aim of the research project is to offer an up-to-date overview of the *status quo* of 4 fundamental procedural rights in criminal proceedings in the EU Member States:

- The right to information,
- The right to legal advice,
- The right to legal assistance free of charge,
- The right to translation and interpretation of documents

First, this report offers an analysis of these procedural rights which the European Convention on Human Rights provides for, as dealt with in recent case law of the European Court of Human Rights.
The underlying reason for this separate analysis is to give an overview of the minimum standards that should be respected in every single EU Member State today and to provide the normative framework to analyse the outcome of the data that has been gathered.

Subsequently, the following part of this report will paint a picture of the extent to which these procedural rights are guaranteed in the formal legislation of each EU Member State. This overview was obtained through an extensive questionnaire[10] which was sent out to all 27 EU Member States. The specific aim of the questionnaire was to obtain up-to-date information on the same subjects as covered by the previous research carried out by Spronken and Attinger and to gain insight in the level of legal protection offered to suspects and accused in the EU Member States. Furthermore, the questionnaire included questions on how the examined procedural rights are dealt with in the Member States within procedures concerning the European Arrest Warrant (EAW) and other mutual recognition instruments. Therefore, the questionnaire was divided into the following chapters:

Chapter 1: The right to legal advice
Chapter 2: The right to legal assistance (partially) free of charge
Chapter 3: The right to translation of documents and the right to interpretation
Chapter 4: Other fundamental guarantees and the right to be informed on them
Chapter 5: European Arrest Warrant and other mutual recognition instruments

In the analysis of the results of the questionnaire, readers will find that "the right to information" was dealt with in the questionnaire as an overarching horizontal issue and not as a separate right, as is the case for the analysis of the ECtHR-case law. The right to information has several dimensions. First of all, it contains the right of anyone charged with a criminal offence to be informed on the nature and cause of the accusations against him and to have access to the evidence on which these accusations are based (the right to information as guaranteed by Art. 6 ECHR). Secondly, the right to information in this research also comprises the right to be informed on fundamental procedural rights. This right to be informed on procedural rights in itself is not covered by the ECHR, but is highly relevant for procedural rights that are mentioned in the ECHR to be practical and effective. Chapter 4 of the questionnaire covers the right to be informed on the charge, on the right to have access to the file, on the right to remain silent and on the right to call witnesses. The right to information on other procedural rights (the right to legal advice, the right to legal assistance (partially) free of charge and the right to translation and interpretation) was dealt with separately in chapter 1, 2, and 3 of the questionnaire.

The questionnaire was sent out to representatives of the Ministries of Justice of the EU Member States in April 2009. Each Member State has named one person responsible for answering the questionnaire.[11] Responses were received between April and July 2009 from all Member States except for Malta. Therefore, this

---

[10] See annex 1.
[11] A list of the relevant contact persons can be found in Section 5 of the report.

report covers information on 26 Member States and no information on Malta could be incorporated.

The replies to the questionnaire are based on formal legislation. However, the respondents were asked to indicate if – to their knowledge – a certain legal provision is not applied in practice or if certain actions covered by this questionnaire are carried out in practice but do not have a legal basis.

The replies to the questionnaire could be filled in on-line. The questions were designed as much as possible as "closed questions" with limited options for answering them. Tick boxes were used which sometimes contained alternative answers (indicated by the words 'choose one of the following answers') whereas sometimes more than one answer was possible (indicated by the words 'check any that apply'). Where relevant, the respondents were asked to refer to the relevant legal basis (statute, secondary legislation et cetera) and provide a translation into English of the text of the legal provision. Also, the respondents were asked to clarify their answers where relevant (indicated by the words 'please specify').

The conclusions drawn up in this report are based on the answers as provided by the representatives of the Ministries of Justice of the Member States. It is important to note that the project team has not carried out any research on the accuracy of these answers. However, when processing the replies to the questionnaire, the project team noticed that in some instances the answers provided were not consistent with the contents of the – according to the respondents – relevant legal provisions. Furthermore, sometimes specifications of answers clarified that the question was misinterpreted or misunderstood. Where relevant such discrepancies have been indicated in the analysis of the answers.

The text of the complete questionnaire and the User Guide (providing for more detailed information on how to use the online questionnaire) are attached to this report under Annex 1. An overview of all diagrams presenting the results of the answers to the questionnaire is attached under Annex 2. The complete answers to the questionnaire are presented in Annex 3 that will be made available on line: http://arno.unimaas.nl/show.cgi?fid=16315

2 Four Fundamental Procedural Rights in Criminal Proceedings throughout the European Union

This chapter provides a comprehensive overview of ECtHR case law on the 4 fundamental rights that are the subject of this study.[12]

2.1 Right to information

2.1.1 *Situations giving rise to the right to information*

The right to information is considered to be a crucial aspect of the overall right to defend oneself. At the level of the ECHR both arrested and not arrested persons are entitled to receive information on the nature and cause of the accusation against them.[13] Additionally, in case of an arrest, the reasons for his arrest become subject to the right to information.[14]

2.1.2 *Timing*

Both Art. 5, 3 and 6, 3, a) ECHR require information to be delivered promptly. No further specification is made. Similarly, the Proposed Framework Decision referred in its Art. 14.1 to an immediate right.

2.1.3 *Means*

The ECHR does not give any indication as to the means to be used to provide the information. The ECHR prefers written to oral information and thus has suggested in its 2003 Green Paper that Member States should be required to inform suspects and defendants by means of a 'Letter of Rights'[15]. Subsequently a similar provision is found in the 2004 proposal.

---

[12] This chapter is a revision and update of the first chapter of the study performed by T.N.B.M. Spronken and M. Attinger, Procedural Rights in criminal proceedings: Existing Level of Safeguards in the European Union, funded and published by the European Commission, 12 December 2005 <http://arno.unimaas.nl/show.cgi?fid=3891>.
[13] Art. 5, 3 and Art. 6, 3, a ECHR.
[14] Art. 5, 3 ECHR.
[15] Green Paper, section 8.1.

2.1.4 Content

- *Accusations and charges*

Even though both Art. 5 and 6 ECHR are fairly specific in the information they require, they are limited to factual information of the case, being reasons for the arrest and the nature and cause of the accusation and the respective legal bases[16]. Information should be provided in a language the defendant understands. The amount of information available for the suspect or accused is strongly dependant on the nature and complexity of the case.

- *Procedural rights*

Regrettably, there is no special provision in the ECHR that the suspect should be notified immediately of the other defence rights enlisted in the Convention (e.g. the right to consult a lawyer, to examine or have examined witnesses, the right to interpretation and translation). According to the EC however, it is important for both the investigating authorities and the persons being investigated to be fully aware of what rights exist. A Letter of rights in a language the suspect understands, does not create new rights but is an efficient way of informing suspects of their rights, which, according to the case law of the ECtHR, are not meant to be only theoretical but also to be effective in practice. Therefore Art. 14.3 of the Proposed Framework Decision required all Member States to "ensure that police stations keep the text of the written notification in all the official Community languages so as to be able to offer an arrested person a copy in a language he understands." From recent case law of the ECtHR can be derived that the state has a duty to take all reasonable steps to make a suspect fully aware of his rights of defence and that domestic authorities have to ensure actively that a suspect understands these rights. [17]

- *Information on the investigation*

Art. 6, 3, b) stipulates that everyone charged with a criminal offence is entitled to have adequate time and facilities for the preparation of his defence. These rights entail the right to have access to all elements that are useful to prepare the defence[18], including information *à décharge* (exculpatory), found by the prosecuting party[19]. Nevertheless, the European Court has accepted the *Public Interest Immunity* for certain elements: the right to full disclosure was not

---

[16] ECtHR 18 March 2008, *Ladent*, (no. 11036/03), § 66; ECtHR 19 December 1960, *Ofner* (no. 524/59), § 5.

[17] ECtHR 11 December 2008, *Panovits* (no. 4268/04), § 68 and § 72; ECtHR 27 March 2007, *Talat Tunç* (no. 32432/96), § 61; ECtHR 10 August 2006, *Padalov* (no. 54784/00), § 52-54.

[18] ECtHR, 14 December 1981, *Jespers* (no. 8403/78).

[19] ECtHR, 16 December 1992, *Edwards* (no. 13071/87), § 35-38.

absolute and could, in pursuit of a legitimate aim such as the protection of national security or of vulnerable witnesses or sources of information, be subject to limitations.[20] Any such restriction on the rights of the defence should, however, be strictly proportionate and counterbalanced by procedural safeguards adequate to compensate for the handicap imposed on the defence. The need for disclosure or non disclosure should at all times be under assessment by the trial judge.[21]

2.2 Right to legal advice

2.2.1 *Seek legal advice or defend oneself*

According to the European Commission, the right to legal advice is a second key issue in procedural rights for suspects. A suspect who is represented by a lawyer is in a far better position with regards to the enforcement of all his other rights, partly because he is better informed of those rights and partly because a lawyer will assist him in ensuring that his rights are respected.[22] The right to legal assistance is covered by other European and international treaties and charters as well; for instance the ICCPR[23], the Universal Declaration of Human Rights[24], the Charter on Fundamental Rights in the European Union[25], the American Convention on Human Rights[26], the African Charter on Human Rights and Peoples Rights[27] and the 1990 UN-resolution on Basic Principles on the Role of Lawyers.[28]

---

[20] ECtHR, 16 February 2000, *Jasper* (no. 27052/95) § 43.

[21] ECtHR, 16 February 2000, *Rowe and Davis* (no. 28901/95), § 58.

[22] Green Paper, section 4.1.

[23] Art. 14 (§ 3, b and d) ICCPR which covers almost the same as Art. 6 ECHR, adding the right to be informed of his right to legal assistance.

[24] In Art. 11 of the Universal Declaration on Human Rights it is determined that everyone being accused of having committed a crime, has the right to have all the guarantees necessary for his defence at his disposal.

[25] Art. 47 CFREU (Right to an effective remedy and to a fair trial).

[26] Art. 8 (§ 2, c – e) of the American Convention on Human Rights covers the same guarantees as Art. 6 ECHR, but adds the right 'to communicate freely and privately with his counsel'.

[27] The African Charter on Human Rights and Peoples Rights also guarantees in Art. 7 (§ 1, c) the right to legal advice, including the right to be advised by a lawyer of his own choice.

[28] In this respect the UN-resolution on 'Basic Principles on the Role of Lawyers' - adopted by the Eight Crime Congress, Havana, 7 September 1990, ratified by Resolution 45/121 of the General Assembly of the UN dated 14 December 1990 - is also of great importance. The ground rules of the rights and duties of lawyers are prescribed in this resolution, emphasising the obligation of the government to guarantee the independence of the legal profession. Freedom of speech and association and assembly of lawyers should be respected and governments have to recognise that the communication between lawyers and clients is confidential. The government also has to guarantee that lawyers have access to the file and information at the earliest possible stage in the proceedings.

In the explanatory note on the 2004 proposal, criminal proceedings were defined as 'all proceedings taking place within the European Union aiming to establish the guilt or innocence of a person suspected of having committed a criminal offence or to decide on the outcome following a guilty plea in respect of a criminal charge'.[29] Legal advice before answering any questions in relation to the charge should protect the suspect against making statements without understanding the legal implications that he (or she) subsequently regrets.[30]

The right to legal advice/assistance is covered by Art. 6 (§ 3, b and c) ECHR. Art. 6 (§ 3 b) stipulates the right of every suspect to have the necessary time and facilities at his disposal to prepare his defence properly. The duration of this "necessary time" is not specified as it is strongly dependant on the complexity of each individual case. However, assigning a new duty lawyer only a few hours before the start of the trial clearly violates the right to have the necessary time to prepare a defence.[31] According to Art. 6, § 3, c, the suspect has the right to choose either to defend himself (however he cannot be coerced into waiving his right to counsel)[32], to be assisted by a lawyer of his own choosing (therefore the denial of legal assistance constitutes a violation[33], as does the failure to allow confidential communication[34]), or to have a lawyer assigned to him in case he does not have the means to pay for a lawyer himself.[35] Art. 6 § 3 (c) does not specify the manner of exercising this right. It thus leaves to the Contracting States the choice of the means of ensuring that it is secured in their judicial systems, the Court's task being only to ascertain whether the method they have chosen is consistent with the requirements of a fair trial.[36]

The right to seek legal representation does not constitute a waiver of the right to personal participation during the trial.

The guarantees laid down in Art. 6 (§ 3) ECHR are not an end in themselves, but must be interpreted in the light of their function in the overall context of the proceedings.[37]

---

[29] The 2004 proposal, section 32.
[30] The 2004 proposal, section 55, see also ECtHR, Grand Chamber, 27 November 2008, *Salduz* (no. 36391/02), § 54.
[31] ECtHR 7 October 2008, *Bogumil*, (no. 35228/03), § 48; ECtHR 9 June 1998, *Twalib*, Reports, 1998.
[32] ECtHR 12 June 2008, *Yaremenko*, (no. 32092/02), § 81.
[33] ECtHR 22 July 2008, *Panasenko*, (no. 10418/03), § 54; ECtHR 26 June 2008, *Shulepov* (no. 15435/03), § 39.
[34] ECtHR 27 November 2007, *Zagaria*, (no. 58295/00), § 36.
[35] ECtHR 11 November 2008, *Timergaliyev*, (no. 40631/02), § 59; ECtHR 10 August 2006, *Padalov* (no. 54784/00), § 53-54.
[36] ECtHR 27 April 2006, *Sannino* (no. 30961/03), § 48.
[37] ECtHR 12 July 1984, *Can* (B 79), § 48. "The court sees it as its task to ascertain whether the proceedings considered as a whole were fair", which is standard case law of the ECtHR, see for

2.2.2 Obligation to provide legal assistance

Notwithstanding the fact that the suspect is entitled to defend himself, obligatory legal representation can be prescribed under certain circumstances, for example when an appeal is lodged.[38] Other circumstances, which are not mentioned in ECtHR case law in relation to obligatory legal advice, were cited in Art. 3 of the 2004 proposal. The obligation to provide legal advice when the suspect is the subject of a European Arrest Warrant, extradition request or other surrender proceedings is an extension of existing provisions.

2.2.3 Effective legal advice

One of the basic obligations of a lawyer is to assist his client, not only in the preparation of the trial itself, but also in the control of the legality of any measures taken in the course of the investigation proceedings.[39] Additionally, this legal assistance has to be effective and the State is under the obligation to ensure that the lawyer has the information necessary to conduct a proper defence.[40] If legal representation is ineffective, the State is obliged to provide the suspect with another lawyer.[41]

Yet the ECtHR has clearly held that the lawyer's conduct is essentially an affair between the lawyer and his client. This is an important recognition by the ECtHR of the independence of the lawyer.[42] This independence is threatened when the State is held responsible for every lawyer's shortcomings. The suspect should not be burdened with the risk of ineffective legal representation. Therefore the ECtHR has held that 'States are required to intervene only if a failure by counsel to provide effective representation is manifest or sufficiently brought to their attention'.[43] The suspect does not have to prove that he has

---

example ECtHR 20 November 1989, *Kostovski*, A 166, § 39 and ECtHR 16 December 1992, *Edwards* (A 247-B), § 34.

[38] ECtHR 24 November 1986, *Gillow* (A 109); ECtHR 25 September 1992, *Croissant* (A 237-B); ECtHR 14 January 2003, *Lagerblom* (no. 26891/95).

[39] ECtHR 12 July 1984, *Can* (B 79); ECtHR 4 March 2003, *Öcalan*, (no. 63486/00).

[40] ECtHR 9 April 1984, *Goddi (A 76)*; ECtHR 4 March 2003, *Öcalan*, (no. 63486/00).

[41] ECtHR 13 May 1980, *Artico* (A 37).

[42] ECtHR 24 November 1993, *Imbrioscia*, (A 275), § 41: "However that may be, the applicant did not at the outset have the necessary legal support, but 'a state cannot be held responsible for every shortcoming on the part of a lawyer appointed for legal purposes'. (...) Owing to the legal professions' independence, the conduct of the defence is essentially a matter between the defendant and his representative; under Art. 6 (§ 3c) the contracting States are required to intervene only if a failure by counsel to provide effective representation is manifest or sufficiently brought to their attention".

[43] ECtHR 24 November 1993, *Imbrioscia* (A 275), § 41, ECtHR 10 October 2002, *Czekalla*, Recueil/Reports 2002, § 65; ECtHR 7 October 2008, *Bogumil*, (no. 35228/03).

been prejudiced due to lack of effective legal assistance[44], nor is it necessary that damages have arisen.[45]

The suspect cannot be expected to assess the effectiveness of his legal representation himself; hence the need for Member States to introduce a monitoring system.[46] This last provision is not stipulated in the ECHR, although the right to effective legal assistance can be deduced from ECtHR case law.

2.2.4   Contact and Consultation

The right to legal representation – and thus to contact a legal advisor – arises immediately upon arrest, although a reasonable time is allowed for the lawyer to arrive.[47] With regard to the moment the right arises, the proposed Framework Decision had stipulated in its Art. 2 that 'a suspected person had the right to legal advice as soon as possible and throughout the criminal proceedings if he wishes to receive it'.

No specification is made as to the circumstances in which consultation should be possible. The latter is not included *expressis verbis* in ECHR, but is considered to be a part of the right in Art. 6.[48] The ECtHR has elaborated on the consultation circumstances in its case law. It has ruled that fair trial was compromised when the consultation could only take place in the presence of a prison guard[49], in the presence of police officers[50] or if a suspect can only communicate with his lawyer separated by a glass partition.[51] Nevertheless, certain security measures could be allowed if proven truly necessary.[52]

2.2.5   Legal advice during police interrogation

The physical presence of a lawyer can provide the necessary counterbalance against pressure used by the police during interviews.[53] When the suspect has to

---

[44] ECtHR 13 May 1980, *Artico* (A 37).
[45] ECtHR 19 February 1991, *Alimena* (A 195-D).
[46] Proposed FD, section 59.
[47] ECtHR 8 February 1996, *John Murray* (Reports 1996-I).
[48] Commission, 12 June 1984, *Can v Austria* (no. 9300/82).
[49] ECtHR 29 November 1991, *S. v Switzerland*, (no. 13965/88).
[50] ECtHR 13 January 2009, *Rybacki* (no. 52479/99, § 53-62.
[51] ECtHR 19 December 2006, *Oferta Plus SRL* (no. 14385/04), § 145-156; ECtHR 13 March 2007, *Castravet*, (no. 23393/05), § 59-60.
[52] ECtHR 31 January 2002, *Lanz* (no. 24430/94).
[53] ECtHR 6 June 2000, *Magee* (no. 28135/95) and ECtHR 2 May 2000, *Codron* (no. 35718/97): "The fact that an accused person who is questioned under caution is assured access to legal advice, and in the applicants' case the physical presence of a solicitor during police interview must be considered a particularly important safeguard for dispelling any compulsion to speak which may be inherent in the terms of the caution. For the court, particular caution is required when a domestic court seeks to attach weight to the fact that a person who is arrested in connection

make decisions during police interrogations that may be decisive for the further course of the proceedings, he has the right to consult a lawyer prior to these interrogations.[54]

Nevertheless, for years the ECtHR held that the right to have a lawyer present during police interrogation could in general not be derived from Art. 6 (§ 3) ECHR.[55] In contradiction to that initial view of the ECtHR, both the Yugoslavia Tribunal[56] and the European Committee for the Prevention of Torture and Inhuman or Degrading Treatment or Punishment (CPT) [57] acknowledged that the right to have a lawyer present during police interrogation is one of the fundamental safeguards against ill-treatment of detained persons. Subsequently this consideration was acknowledged in Art. 2 (§ 2) of the 2004 proposal.

However, in 2 recent judgments the ECtHR has underlined the importance of the investigation stage for the preparation of the criminal proceedings, and referred to the recommendations of the CPT. "The Court finds that in order for the right to a fair trial to remain sufficiently 'practical and effective' Art. 6 § 1 requires that, as a rule, access to a lawyer should be provided as from the first interrogation of a suspect by the police, unless it is demonstrated in the light of the particular circumstances of each case that there are compelling reasons to restrict this right." The ECtHR further indicates that even where compelling reasons may exceptionally justify denial of access to a lawyer, such restriction may not unduly prejudice the rights of the accused. As a consequence the ECtHR considers that the lack of legal assistance during a suspect's interrogation would constitute a restriction of his defence rights and that these rights will in principle be irretrievably prejudiced when incriminating statements, made

---

with a criminal offence and who has not been given access to a lawyer does not provide detailed responses when confronted with questions the answers to which may be incriminating." (§ 60).

[54] ECtHR 6 June 2000, *Averill* (no. 36408/97).

[55] In *Dougan* (ECtHR 14 December 1999, no. 44738/98) the ECtHR held: "Before the Court of Appeal they argued for the first time that the statements made by the applicant to the police should have been declared inadmissible on account of the absence of a solicitor during interview. However the merits of that argument must be tested against the circumstances of the case. Quite apart from the consideration that this line of defence should have been used at first instance, the Court considers that an applicant cannot rely on Art. 6 to claim the right to have a solicitor physically present during interview." See also ECtHR 16 October 2001, *Brennan* (no. 39846/98).

[56] Art. 18 (§ 3) Statute of the International Tribunal for the former Yugoslavia (ICTY). Decision on the Defence Motion to Exclude Evidence from ICTY in Zdravko Mucic, 2 September 1997, Case No. IT-96-21-T, Trial Chamber II.

[57] 2nd General report (CPT/Inf (92) 3), sections 36-38.

during police interrogation without access to a lawyer, are used for a conviction.[58]

This new interpretation of Art. 6 § 3 (c), also referred to as the 'Salduz doctrine', has been confirmed in several judgments. In this (post-Salduz) case law the ECtHR has convicted the defending States (often Turkey) by merely referring to the Salduz principle and adding that no exceptional circumstances were present that could justify an exception to this jurisprudence.[59] Moreover, in the case of Shabelnik v. Ukraine of 19 February 2009 the ECtHR has made a clear stance as regards the interpretation that should be given to its new jurisprudence: *"...the applicant, having been warned about criminal liability for refusal to testify and at the same time having been informed about his right not to testify against himself, could have been confused, as he alleged, about his liability for refusal to testify, especially in the absence of legal advice during that interview".*[60]

---

[58] ECtHR, Grand Chamber, 27 November 2008, *Salduz* (no. 36391/02), § 54-55 and ECtHR 11 December 2008, *Panovits* (no. 4268/04), § 66 and 70-73.

[59] ECtHR, 10 March 2009, *Böke and Kandemir* (71912/01; 26968/02 and 36397/03); ECtHR, 3 March 2009, *Aba* (no. 7638/02 and 24146/04); ECtHR, 17 February 2009, *Aslan and Demir* (no. 38940/02 and 5197/03); ECtHR, 17 February 2009, *Oztürk* (no. 16500/04).

[60] ECtHR 19 February 2009, Shabelnik (application number 16404/03).

2.3   Right to legal assistance free of charge

The right to free legal aid is not unconditional. Art. 6 (§ 3c) ECRM stipulates that a suspect has the right to free legal aid on 2 conditions, namely if (1) he does not have sufficient means to pay for legal assistance and (2) when the interests of justice so require. The ECtHR holds that the suspect does not have to prove 'beyond all doubt' that he lacks the means to pay for his defence.[61] The Proposed Framework Decision stipulated in Art. 5 that the costs of legal advice should be borne in whole or in part by the Member States if these costs would cause undue financial hardship to the suspected person or his dependents. The ECtHR indicates 3 factors which should be taken into account[62]:

- The seriousness of the offence and the severity of the potential sentence,
- The complexity of the case, and
- The social and personal situation of the defendant.

The right to free legal aid exists whenever the deprivation of liberty is at stake[63], narrowing down the definition of 'interests of justice'. Denying free legal aid for a period during which procedural acts, including questioning of the applicants and their medical examinations, are carried out is unacceptable according to the ECtHR.[64]

Member States are free to operate the system that appears to them to be the most effective as long as free legal advice remains available where the interests of justice demand it.[65]

---

[61] ECtHR 25 April 1983, *Pakelli* (A, 64, § 34).
[62] ECtHR 24 May 1991, *Quaranta* (A, 205, § 35).
[63] ECtHR 10 June 1996, *Benham (Reports 1996-III).*
[64] ECtHR 20 June 2002, *Berlinski* (no. 27715/95 and 30209/96).
[65] The 2004 proposal, section 60-61.

2.4   Right to interpretation and translation

Suspects who do not speak or understand the language of the proceedings are clearly at a disadvantage. They are especially vulnerable, whatever their circumstances. Consequently, the right to interpretation and translation strikes the Commission as particularly important.[66]

2.4.1   The scope of the right to interpretation and translation

-    *All parts of criminal proceedings*

The right to free interpretation is derived from Art. 5,2 and 6,3,a-e ECHR[67] and established in ECtHR case law.[68] It extends to all parts of the criminal proceedings, which means that Member States have to provide an interpreter as soon as possible after it has come to light that the suspect is in need of an interpreter[69]. The fact that no 'registered' interpreter was present during an initial police interrogation does not compromise the right to a fair trial and interpretation, as long as the interpretation was sufficient in quality and scope.[70] The ultimate duty to ensure fairness of the proceedings rests with the trial judge[71], since he is the ultimate guardian of the fairness of the proceedings.[72] The 2004 proposal referred to a competent authority being in charge of the decision regarding which documents need to be translated.

-    *Translation of written documents*

The right to free translation of documents is not explicitly mentioned in Art. 6 ECHR. It is however established in ECtHR case law and incorporated by the EC in the 2004 proposal. The ECtHR held that only those documents, which the defendant 'needs to understand in order to have a fair trial', need to be translated:

The right, stated in paragraph 3 (e) of Art. 6 (Art. 6-3-e), to the free assistance of an interpreter applies not only to oral statements made at the trial hearing but also to documentary material and the pre-trial proceedings. Paragraph 3 (e) (Art. 6-3-e)

---

[66] Green Paper, section 5.2.

[67] This is also covered by Art. 14 § 3, a and f ICCPR and Art. 55 and 67 of the Rome Statute. The Rome Statute provides in Art. 55 the right to an interpreter and a translator for persons under investigation. Art. 67 of the Rome Statute provides for interpretation and translation at trial.

[68] ECtHR 28 November 1978, *Luedicke, Belkacem and Koç* (A 29).

[69] The 2004 proposal, section 63.

[70] ECtHR 19 December 1989, *Kamasinksi* (A 168) § 76-77; See also the 2004 proposal, section 67.

[71] Green Paper, section 5.2.1 (a).

[72] ECtHR 24 September 2002, *Cuscani* (no. 32771/96); ECtHR 18 October 2006, *Hermi* (no. 18114/02), § 69-71.

signifies that a person "charged with a criminal offence" who cannot understand or speak the language used in court has the right to the free assistance of an interpreter for the translation or interpretation of all those documents or statements in the proceedings instituted against him which it is necessary for him to understand or to have rendered into the court's language in order to have the benefit of a fair trial (see the Luedicke, Belkacem and Koç judgment of 28 November 1978, Series A no. 29, p. 20, § 48).

However, paragraph 3 (e) (Art. 6-3-e) does not go so far as to require a written translation of all items of written evidence or official documents in the procedure. The interpretation assistance provided should be such as to enable the defendant to have knowledge of the case against him and to defend himself, notably by being able to put before the court his version of the events.[73]

The rules on how much material is to be translated vary according to the Member State and the nature of the case. According to the EC, this variation is acceptable as long as the proceedings remain 'fair'.[74] The onus should be on the defence lawyer to ask for translations of any documents he considers necessary over and above what is provided by the prosecution.[75]

An indictment plays a crucial role in the criminal process, in that it is from the moment of its service that the defendant is formally put on written notice of the factual and legal basis of the charges against him. A defendant not conversant with the court's language may in fact be put at a disadvantage if he is not also provided with a written translation of the indictment in a language he understands. The fact that only the titles of the crimes alleged are translated, but not the material substance upon which the charges were grounded, does not necessarily constitute a breach of the right to information and interpretation, when the facts are not so complicated and an oral explanation sufficiently informs the accused of 'the nature and cause of the accusation against him', for the purposes of paragraph 3 (a) of Art. 6 (Art. 6-3-a).[76]

---

[73] ECtHR 19 December 1989, *Kamasinksi* (A 168); see also ECtHR 14 January 2003, *Lagerblom* (no. 26891/95).
[74] Green Paper, section 5.2.1 (c).
[75] The 2004 proposal, section 66.
[76] ECtHR 19 December 1989, *Kamasinksi* (A 168) § 81.

-   Hearing or speech impairment

The rights granted in Art. 6 can also require hearing aid during trial, when a persons' hearing impairment significantly reduces the ability to follow the proceedings.[77]

2.4.2   Free interpretation and translation

Both Art. 5, 2 and 6,3 ECHR combine to the importance of the information being provided in a language the accused understands, with a right to free translation and interpretation. Similarly, Art. 6 and 7 of the 2004 proposal entailed the right to free interpretation and the right to free translation of all relevant documents.[78]

2.4.3   Accuracy of the translation and interpretation

The interpretation should enable the defendant's 'effective participation' in the proceedings. The proceedings should be recorded as a method of verifying that the interpretation was accurate. Recordings should not be used to challenge the proceedings from any other point of view.[79]

Whilst Member States are conscious of these obligations in theory, these are not complied with in full in practice.[80] The difficulty however, is not one of acceptance on the part of the Member States, but one of levels and means of provision, and perhaps most importantly, costs of implementation.[81]

-   Registers of translators and interpreters

In order to comply with the provision on accurate translation and interpretation, research[82] has shown that a training system for translators is essential. The training system should focus on general practice of   interpretation   and translation and specific practice of the legal system. According to this study, Member States which currently do not have any training system should be required to develop one. As guaranteeing the quality of the training is of real

---

[77] ECtHR 14 October 2008, *Timergaliyev*, (no. 40631/02), § 60.

[78] ECtHR 28 November 1978, *Luedicke* (no. 6210/73).

[79] The 2004 proposal, section 69 and 70.

[80] The 2004 proposal, section 36 - In some cases even a prisoner's cellmate is used as an interpreter. See also Reflection Forum on Multilingualism and Interpreter Training March 2009 <http://ec.europa.eu./commission_barosso/orban/docs/FinalL_Reflection_Forum_Report_en.pdf>.

[81] Green Paper, section 5.2.

[82] The research was carried out by the Lessius Hogeschool with the aid of a European Commission 'Grotius' subsidy (Grotius II project 2001/GRP/015); see also Heleen Keijzer-Lambooy, Willem Jan Gasille, (eds.) Instruments for Lifting Language Barriers in Intercultural Legal Proceedings EU project JAI/2003/AGIS/048, ITV Hogeschool voor Tolken en Vertalers 2005.

importance, according to the study, standards should be governed and accredited by an independent body. This accreditation must be renewed on a regular basis, to maintain skills and continuous professional development. Furthermore, a register should be made, listing all accredited interpreters and translators, and should be easily accessible to courts and legal practitioners. In this regard, it is important to stress that interpretation and translation are 2 different professions which should be treated accordingly. Consequently 2 different registers are required.[83]

- *Special attention for uncommon languages*

Another difficulty is the translation and interpretation of uncommon languages. It is for the Member States to make arrangements to cover such languages.[84] Member States must make funds available to make court interpretation and translation a more attractive career option to language graduates. Also, law graduates with excellent language skills should be encouraged to join the profession and be offered appropriate training.[85] Member States should also make an effort to recruit a sufficient number of translators and interpreters.[86]

---

[83] C. Morgan, 'The Commission's draft proposal for a Framework Decision on certain procedural rights applying in proceedings in criminal matters throughout the European Union' in: Heleen Keijzer-Lambooy, Willem Jan Gasille, (eds.) Instruments for Lifting Language Barriers in Intercultural Legal Proceedings, p. 27 – 28. See also the Green Paper, section 5.2.2 (a).
[84] Green Paper, section 5.2.2 (c).
[85] Green Paper, section 5.2.2 (d).
[86] Green Paper, section 5.2.2 (e).

3 Analysis of the replies of Member States to the questionnaire

3.1 The Right to Legal Advice

3.1.1 Contact

In all Member States – except for one (the Netherlands) – the right to contact a lawyer (or legal representative) after arrest is guaranteed. In the majority of these countries (17) the right to contact a lawyer can be effected immediately after arrest while in some countries (7) this is possible at a certain stage of investigation or the proceedings (diagram 2).

However, there may be limitations to the right to contact a lawyer. For example, in Austria – whenever it appears necessary to avoid any impairment of the proceedings or the evidence – the right may be (temporarily) limited. A serious reason to restrict the contact in this context means for example, if the suspect is (suspected of being) a member of a criminal organization and the other members are not yet arrested. An important guarantee that the suspect is able to benefit from legal assistance at an early stage of the proceedings is laid down in Hungarian legislation: when assistance of a defence lawyer is mandatory and the detained suspect has not retained a lawyer, he will be appointed one by the prosecutor, the court or the investigating authority no later than the first interrogation.

In one Member State (Belgium) the right to contact a lawyer can be effected within a certain lapse of time after arrest. In Belgium the arrested person has to be heard by the investigating judge within 24 hours after the arrest and the right to contact a lawyer starts after this hearing.

Diagram 2. When can the right to contact a lawyer (or legal representative) after the arrest be effected?

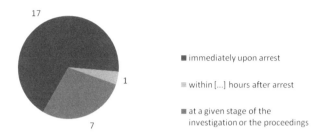

Immediately upon arrest: BG; CY; CZ; EE; FI; FR; EL; IT; LV; LT; PL; PT; RO; SK; SI; ES; UK

At a given stage of the investigation or the proceedings: AT; DE; DK; HU; IE; LU; SE

Within […] hours after arrest: BE

In all Member States where the right to contact a lawyer after arrest is guaranteed, there is a legal obligation to inform the suspect on this right. Also, it is guaranteed that this information is provided in a language the suspect understands. In the majority of countries, the obligation to inform the suspect arises promptly after arrest. In some Member States (8), this duty arises at a given stage of the investigation or the proceedings, such as before the first interrogation of the suspect. In Belgium the investigating judge, who hears the suspect within 24 hours after arrest, has to inform him at that time of his right to contact a lawyer (diagram 4).

With regard to the way in which the suspect should be informed on his right to contact a lawyer, it turns out that in the majority of countries (16) this information is only provided orally.[87] However, in some Member States this is done in writing (5) or both orally and in writing (4). Only in England and Wales the right to contact a lawyer is mentioned in a letter of rights (diagram 5)[88].

---

[87] Sometimes, as for example in Romania, the fact that this information was provided to the suspect should be written down in an official record that is added to the case file.
[88] Within the context of the questionnaire a letter of rights was understood to mean 'written information on the suspect's procedural rights in a standardised form'.

Diagram 4. When does the duty to inform the suspect of the right to contact a lawyer arise?

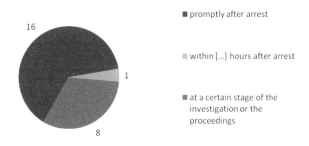

Promptly after arrest: AT; BG; EE; FI; FR; EL; HU; IT; LV; LT; PL; PT; SK; SI; ES; UK
At a certain stage of the investigation or the proceedings: CY; CZ; DK; DE; IE; LU; RO; SE
Within […] hours after arrest: BE

Diagram 5. How should the suspect be informed of the right to contact a lawyer? (more than one answer possible)

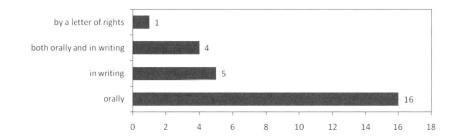

By a letter of rights: UK **Both orally and in writing:** AT; CZ; LU; PL
In writing: BE; BG; IE; LV; PT
Orally: CY; EE; FI; FR; DE; EL; HU; LT; RO; SK; SI; ES; SE; UK; IT; DK

In the vast majority of Member States it is not possible to limit the right to contact a lawyer after arrest. In 4 countries such a possibility does exist either during a certain amount of time after arrest (varying from 24 hours until 48 hours after arrest) or until a given stage of the investigation or the proceedings (diagram 9). In Greece, the possibility to limit the right to contact a lawyer after arrest is not expressly provided for in the law but it may nevertheless happen in practice in order to better obtain and safeguard the gathering of evidence.

3.1.2   Free choice

In all 26 Member States the suspect has the right to a lawyer of his own choosing. This is often not the case if the lawyer is provided free of charge (see § 3.2.2)

3.1.3   Consultation

In all 26 Member States it is guaranteed that consultation with a lawyer (in person or by telephone) is out of hearing of third parties and/or without its contents being monitored by any technical means. In most cases, this guarantee is laid down in the Constitution and/or regulated by statute. In Greece, although consultation between the suspect and his lawyer may not be monitored by the authorities, this is not expressly laid down in the law.[89]

Furthermore, in the vast majority of Member States (22) it is guaranteed that consultation (in person or by telephone) is possible before questioning by the police. In 4 countries this possibility is not guaranteed (diagram 12).[90]

---

[89] The respondent of the Greek Ministry of Justice did not mention whether this practice is specified somewhere.

[90] From additional information provided by one of these countries – the Netherlands – it follows that as a result of recent Strasbourg case law (Salduz and Panovits case, see § 2.2.5) the Dutch code of criminal procedure will be amended and the right to contact a lawyer before being questioned by the police will be explicitly included as well as the obligation to inform the suspect of this right. Requested to give an interpretation of the consequences of the ECtHR judgments for the Dutch practice the Supreme Court of the Netherlands ruled on 30 June 2009 that a suspect has the right to consult a lawyer before the first police interrogation, but that only a juvenile suspect has the right to also have a lawyer present during police interrogation (HR 30 June 2009, no. 2411.08 J, NbSr 2009, 249).

Diagram 9. For which period of time is it possible to limit the right to contact a lawyer after arrest?

Up to [...] hours after arrest: FR; EL; UK
Until a certain stage of the proceedings: AT

Diagram 12. Is it guaranteed that consultation (in person or by telephone) is possible before questioning by the police?

No guarantee that consultation is possible before questioning by the police: BE; EL; LV; NL
Yes: AT; BG; CY; CZ; DK; EE; FI; FR; DE; HU; IE; IT; LT; LU; PL; PT; RO; SK; SI; ES; SE; E&W

It is possible for a defence lawyer to visit his client at the police station in all countries, except for one (Belgium). In the majority of Member States (20) the lawyer does not need permission to visit his client at the police station (diagram 14).

In the countries that do require permission, the person or authority who decides on this matter varies. For example in Poland, the lawyer needs the permission of the police officer on duty whereas in Sweden permission may be granted by the leader of the inquiry (investigation), the prosecutor or the court. Also, in most countries (21) these visits at the police station are not limited in time and/or frequency (diagram 15). In 4 countries there are limitations of such kind, as for example in France where the visit is limited in time (a maximum of thirty minutes) or United Kingdom where visits are granted at a time that is convenient to the overall investigation and also at a time practicable to the Duty Officer who has custody, charge and care of all detainees.

Diagram 14. Does the lawyer need permission to visit his client held at the police station?

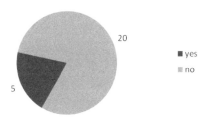

Yes, permission required to visit client at police station: CY; IE; PL; SK; SE

No: AT; BE; BG; CZ; DK; EE; FI; FR; DE; EL; HU; IT; LV; LT; LU; NL; PT; RO; SI; ES; UK

Diagram 15. Are lawyer-client visits at the police station limited in time and/or frequency?

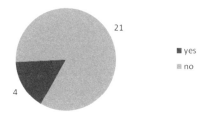

Yes, visits limited in time and/or frequency: FR; IE; SK; UK

No: AT; BG; CY; CZ; DK; EE; FI; DE; EL; HU; IT; LV; LT; LU; NL; PL; PT; RO; SI; ES; SE

It is possible for a defence lawyer to visit the suspect in prison in all countries. In the majority (20) of Member States the lawyer does not need permission for such a visit (diagram 17). In a few countries (6), the lawyer does need permission from a certain authority. For example, in Austria the lawyer needs a formal authentication (during the preliminary proceeding from the public prosecutor and during the trial proceedings from the presiding judge) to visit the suspect remaining in prison. Also, in most countries (22) the lawyer's visits to the suspect in prison are not limited in time and/or frequency (diagram 18). It is important to note that the (4) respondents stating that there are limitations in time and/or frequency do not refer to any specific time and/or frequency limits provided for in national legislation but rather to general limitations connected with the opening hours of the detention facility. Probably such general limitations will apply in most Member States.

Diagram 17. Does the lawyer need permission to visit his client detained in prison?

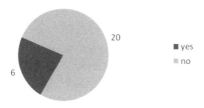

Yes, permission required to visit client detained in prison: AT; CY; PL; SK; SE; UK
No: BE; BG; CZ; DK; EE; FI; FR; DE; EL; HU; IE; IT; LV; LT; LU; NL; PT; RO; SI; ES

Diagram 18. Are lawyer-client visits in prison limited in time and/or frequency?

Yes, visits limited in time and/or frequency: AT; SK; SE; UK
No: BE; BG; CY; CZ; DK; EE; FI; FR; DE; EL; HU; IE; IT; LV; LT; LU; NL; PL; PT; RO; SI; ES

In 9 Member States there is a possibility to supervise the oral communication (including telephone conversations) between the suspect and his lawyer after arrest (diagram 19). In Sweden this possiblity depends on the kind of defence lawyer: supervision of oral communication is only possible if the lawyer is not a public defence counsel. In most countries such supervision has to be ordered by the prosecutor or the (investigating) judge without any specific legal remedies provided to the defence in this respect. In the majority of Member States specific time limits are provided for but these vary widely: from a maximum of 6 days (the Netherlands) to a maximum of 8 months (Spain). Also, the grounds on which such supervision can be ordered vary significantly. In some countries supervision of oral communication is only possible when the lawyer himself is suspected of committing criminal offences while in other Member States there should be a danger of conspiracy or collusion. In a few countries the grounds provided for by law are rather vague: for example in Poland supervision of lawyer-client communication is possible 'where particularly justified', in Spain supervision can be ordered in cases of terrorism and in general by the investigating judge while the law does not specify in what kind of situations. None of the 9 Member States provide for a specific legal remedy for the defence against the supervision of oral communication. Supervision can include listening into telephone conversations, being present at visits from the lawyer, or only supervision of a visit out of hearing (see for more details the answers provided to questions 19a-19e of the Questionnaire).

Also, in 9 of the Member States there is a possibility to supervise the written communication between the suspect and his lawyer after arrest. It should be noted that these are not completely the same 9 countries as mentioned above (allowing supervision of oral communication) (diagram 20). In most countries this kind of supervision is not connected to a fixed time limit nor is a specific legal remedy for the defence provided for

Diagram 19. Are there possibilities to supervise the oral communication (including telephone conversations) between lawyer and suspect after arrest?

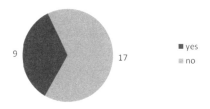

Yes, possibilities to supervise oral communication: AT; BE; NL; PL; RO; SK; ES; SE; UK
No: BG; CY; CZ; DK; EE; FI; FR; DE; EL; HU; IE; IT; LV; LT; LU; PT; SI

Diagram 20. Are there legal possibilities to supervise the written communication between lawyer and suspect after arrest?

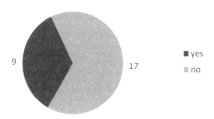

Yes, possibilities to supervise written communication: AT; CY; NL; PL; PT; RO; ES; SE; UK
No: BE; BG; CZ; DK; EE; FI; FR; DE; EL; HU; IE; IT; LV; LT; LU; SK; SI

3.1.4   Questioning

In the majority of Member States the lawyer has the right to be present when the suspect is being questioned (by the police or the prosecutor or the investigating judge or another official such as custom officers, special investigative services, military police, financial crime investigation services). However, in 5 Member States (Belgium, France, Ireland, Scotland and the Netherlands) the lawyer does not have the right to be present at interrogations by the police (diagram 22). With respect to the competences of the lawyer during questioning, it appears that in most countries the lawyer is allowed to make remarks, ask questions and to intervene.

In 6 Member States the lawyer does not have the right to consult with his client in private during interrogation (diagram 23). The Slovak Republic takes a special position in this respect: it is the only country where the lawyer – who is allowed to participate in questioning by the police, the prosecutor and the investigating judge – does not have the right to intervene, ask questions, make remarks nor to consult with his client in private. In the code of criminal procedure of the Slovak Republic it is expressively stated that the suspect is not entitled to consult with his lawyer during questioning on how to answer the question posed.[91]

In nearly all countries allowing the lawyer to be present during (some kind of) questioning there is an obligation for the authorities to inform the suspect of this right. Only in the Netherlands this obligation to inform the suspect does not exist. Furthermore, in all countries (again, except for the Netherlands) there is an obligation to provide the information on the right to have a lawyer present during questioning in a language the suspect understands.

---

[91] According to the answers of the Slovak Republic the lawyer does have 'other competences' during questioning but these were not specified in the answers to the questionnaire.

Diagram 22. Does the right of the lawyer to be present throughout questioning cover...?

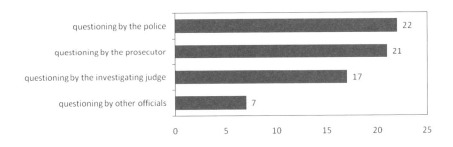

By the police: AT; BG; CY; CZ; DK; EE; FI; DE; EL; HU; IT; LV; LT; LU; PL; PT; RO; SK; SI; ES; SE; E&W

By the prosecutor: AT; BG; CY; CZ; DK; EE; FI; FR; DE; EL; HU; IT; LV; LT; PL; PT; RO; SK; SI; ES; SE

By the investigating judge: CY; CZ; EE; FR; ES; DE; EL; HU; IT; LV; LT; LU; NL; PL; PT; SK; SI

By other officials: AT; BG; CY; FR; LT; PL; SE

Diagram 23. What are the competences of the lawyer during questioning?

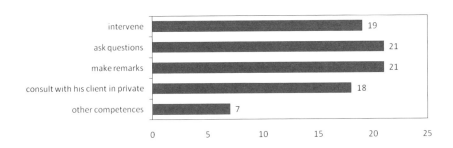

Intervene: BG; CY; CZ; DK; EE; FR; DE; HU; IT; LV; LT; LU; NL; PL; PT; RO; SI; ES; E&W

Ask questions: AT; BG; CZ; DK; EE; FI; FR; DE; HU; IT; LV; LT; LU; NL; PL; PT; RO; SI; ES; SE; E&W

Make remarks: BG; CY; CZ; DK; EE; FR; DE; EL; HU; IT; LV; LT; LU; NL; PL; PT; RO; SI; ES; SE; E&W

Consult with client in private: AT; BG; CY; CZ; DK; EE; FI; FR; DE; EL; HU; IT; PL; PT; SI; ES; SE; E&W

Other competences: BG; CZ; FR; HU; LV; LT; SK

51

The moment at which the obligation to inform the suspect of his right to have a lawyer present during questioning arises, varies. In the majority of Member States (14) the suspect has to be informed of this promptly after arrest. In 9 countries this obligation arises at a given stage of the investigation or the proceedings (diagram 25). In most situations this means (at the latest) before the first interrogation. In a situation where the suspect is informed of his right to have a lawyer present for the first time at the beginning of his first interrogation, this right can obviously only be exercised effectively if he is offered the opportunity to contact a lawyer at that moment and if the interrogation will be postponed. However, only one of the respondents (Lithuania) indicated that the code of criminal procedure expressly states that the authorities are obliged to provide an opportunity for the suspect to exercise his right to defence. For all other countries, it is not clear whether there exists an obligation to give the suspect an opportunity to effectuate (within a reasonable time) his right to be questioned in the presence of his lawyer.

Also, the way in which the suspect should be informed of his right to have a lawyer present during questioning varies (diagram 26). Only in 5 Member States the suspect is informed of this right by means of a letter of rights. In most countries (19) the information is, *inter alia,* provided orally, and in 10 of these 19 countries this is the only way the suspect is informed. In 9 countries the suspect is (also) informed in a written manner. Latvia is the only Member State in which the suspect is only informed in writing.

Diagram 25. When does the duty to inform the suspect of his right to have a lawyer present throughout questioning arise for the first time?

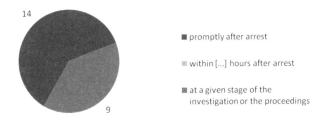

14

9

- promptly after arrest
- within [...] hours after arrest
- at a given stage of the investigation or the proceedings

Promptly after arrest: BG; CY; EE; FI; EL; HU; IT; LV; LU; PT; SK; SI; ES; E&W
At a given stage of the investigation or the proceedings: AT; CZ; DK; FR; DE; LT; PL; RO; SE

Diagram 26. How should the suspect be informed of his right to have a lawyer present during questioning?

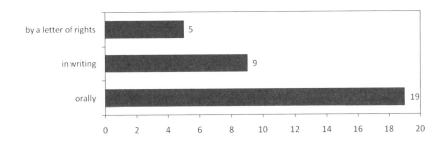

Letter of rights: AT; CZ; LU; PL; SE
In writing: BG; EE; FI; FR; HU; LV; LT; PT; RO
Orally: AT; BG; CY; EE; FI; FR; DE; DK; EL; HU; IT; LT; PT; RO; SK; SI; ES; SE; E&W

In all Member States except for 3 (Portugal, Spain and Italy) the confession made by a suspect in the absence of his lawyer may be used as evidence in court. In this respect, most respondents refer to the free evaluation of evidence by the trial judge as being one of the fundamental principles underlying their criminal justice system. However, in some countries there are limitations to the use of confessions made in the absence of a lawyer. For example in Slovenia, such a confession may only be used as evidence in court if the suspect has (expressly) waived his right to a lawyer. Such a waiver should be noted in the record of the investigation.

With respect to audio- and video recording of the questioning of the suspect it turns out that in the majority of Member States (20) interrogations are sometimes audio recorded. In 6 countries audio recording never occur and in none of the countries are all interrogations being audio recorded (diagram 29).[92] In most countries the parties to the proceedings who have a right to inspect the case file will also have the right to inspect (a transcript of) the audio recording.

In only one Member State – Ireland – all interrogations are being video recorded. In the majority of the other countries (19) this happens sometimes and in 6 Member States video recording of interrogations never occur (diagram 32). When comparing the answers to the questions on audio and video recording it turns out that in 4 countries[93] both ways of recording are never carried out during questioning of suspects.

---

[92] Except for England and Wales where all police interviews are in principle audio recorded. This is not the case in Scotland.
[93] CY; EL; IT; LU.

Diagram 29. Is the questioning of the suspect audio recorded?

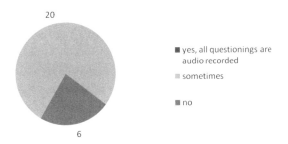

Sometimes: AT; BE; BG; CZ; EE; FI; DE; DK; HU; LV; LT; NL; PL; PT; RO; SK; SI; ES; SE; UK
No audio recording: CY; FR; EL; IE; IT; LU

Diagram 32. Is the questioning of the suspect video recorded?

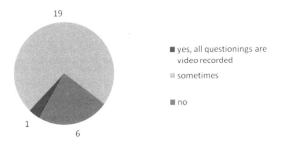

All questioning are video recorded: IE
Sometimes: AT; BE; BG; CZ; DK; EE; FI; FR; HU; LV; LT; NL; PL; PT; SK; SI; ES; SE; UK
No video recording: CY; DE; EL; IT; LU; RO

3.1.5   Conclusions on the right to legal advice

The right to contact a lawyer after arrest exists in most Member States and in most of these countries this right cannot be limited. However, it follows from the analysis of the results of the questionnaire that there is a great divergence as to the moment at which the right to contact a lawyer can be effected. For example, in a considerable number of countries this is not possible immediately after arrest but only at a given stage of the investigation or the proceedings.

Although the obligation to inform the suspect on his right to contact a lawyer exists in all Member States, the actual scope of this legal obligation varies widely. This divergence particularly applies to the moment at which the obligation arises and the manner in which the suspect should be informed. Striking fact is that in only one of the Member States (England and Wales) the right to contact a lawyer is mentioned in a letter of rights.

Visiting clients at police stations and in prison seems to be rather unproblematic throughout the EU: in most countries no permission is required and no limitations in time and/or frequency exist. Although all Member States indicate that it is guaranteed that consultation with a lawyer is out of hearing of third parties and/or without its contents being monitored by any technical means, a considerable number of countries also state that supervision of oral and/or written communication is possible. Striking fact is that there is a wide variety as to the time limits and grounds provided for these forms of supervision. The analysis shows that especially the conditions for supervision of written communication are rather vague, not connected to specific time limits nor are the applicable legal frameworks providing for any specific legal remedies.

With respect to the interrogation of the suspect, the research shows that making video- and/or audio recordings of the questioning is not common practice within the EU. An exception is England and Wales, where interviews with suspects at the police station are always tape recorded and exceptions are only made if it is not reasonably practicable to do so (failure of equipment) or where it is clear from the outset that no prosecution will ensue. In Scotland however this is not a common practice as in most countries where audio or video recording occurs sometimes. In a few countries such recordings are never made.

With regard to legal assistance before and during police interrogation in 4 Member States (Belgium, Greece, Latvia and the Netherlands) the right to consult a lawyer before questioning is not guaranteed. In 5 countries, namely Belgium, France, Ireland, Scotland and the Netherlands, there is no right for the lawyer to be present at interrogations carried out by the police. To conclude; in Greece and Latvia, there is a right for the lawyer to be present during police interrogation but no right to prior consultation, while in France, Ireland and Scotland there is a right to consultation prior to the police interrogation but there is no right for the lawyer to be present during the police interrogation. In Belgium and the Netherlands[94] there is nor a right to prior consultation with a lawyer nor a right for a lawyer to be present during police interrogation.

In almost all countries where the lawyer is allowed to be present during police interrogation, authorities are obliged to inform the suspect of this right. Striking however, is the fact that there are considerable differences among Member States as to the moment at which the obligation to inform the suspect of this right arises and the way in which the information is provided to the suspect. More specifically, although in most countries the suspect should be informed at the latest before his first interrogation it is not clear whether there is an obligation for the authorities to postpone the interrogation when the suspect asks for the presence of his lawyer. If this is not guaranteed, effectively exercising the right to have a lawyer present at the first interrogation will entail serious difficulties. Only in a small number of countries the right to have a lawyer present during questioning is mentioned in a letter of rights. In a considerable number of countries there is no possibility for the defence to deliberate in private during questioning.

Finally, the study shows that the presence of a lawyer at the interrogation is not deemed indispensable: in only 3 Member States it is not allowed to use the confession of a suspect made in the absence of his lawyer as evidence in court.

---

[94] In the Netherlands this has changed as a result of the Salduz judgment of the ECtHR Grand Chamber, 27 November 2008, *Salduz* (no.36391/02). Requested to give an interpretation of the consequences of this judgment for the Dutch practice the Supreme Court of the Netherlands ruled on 30 June 2009 that a suspect has the right to consult a lawyer before the first police interrogation, but that only a juvenile suspect has the right to also have a lawyer present during police interrogation (HR 30 June 2009, no. 2411.08 J, NbSr 2009, 249).

3.2 The Right to Legal Assistance (partially) free of charge

3.2.1 Criteria

In nearly all Member States – except for one (Germany) – the suspect has a right to legal assistance (partially) free of charge.

In the majority of these countries (15) there is a merits test to check whether professional legal aid is in the interest of justice given the particular circumstances of the case and/or the suspect.[95] Specifications of these merits tests vary but in many – especially Central and Eastern European countries – it mainly concerns situations of obligatory defence. In other countries ground for legal assistance (partially) free of charge may be found in the gravity of the case (for example in Ireland a defence lawyer should be appointed in case of a murder charge) or the fact that the suspect is detained (as is the case in the Netherlands). In ten Member States a merits test does not exist (diagram 36).

---

[95] Examples of such particular circumstances are inter alia the fact that the suspect appears not to be able to understand the content or the meaning of the proceedings owing to his age, mental, physical or emotional condition or the fact that he is formally accused of having committed a criminal offence which involves a complex factual or legal situation.

Diagram 36. Is there a merits test to check whether professional legal aid is in the interest of justice?

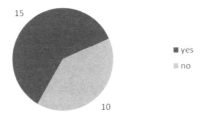

No merits test: BE; DK; FI; FR; IT; LV; LT; LU; PT; SI

Yes: AT; BG; CY; CZ; EE; EL; HU; IE; NL; PL; RO; SK; ES; SE; UK

The majority of Member States (20) providing for legal assistance (partially) free of charge apply a means test.[96] In 5 countries a means test does not exist (diagram 37). There is a considerable variation as to the content and meaning of the means test. In some countries it entails a certain annual or monthly income. In others, the means test is far less specific and based on rather vague legal criteria. For example in the Slovak Republic legal assistance (partially) free of charge is available for the accused 'who does not have sufficient means to cover the legal costs of defence'. Likewise, in Poland the suspect is eligible for legal aid if 'he can duly prove that he is unable to pay the defence costs without prejudice to his and his family's support and maintenance'. There are however no rules established in Poland on how the suspect should prove that he is unable to pay for legal assistance. Equally, no verifiable criteria are mentioned in the answers to the questionnaire on how requests for free legal aid are dealt with in Poland. In Ireland an applicant for legal aid must establish to the satisfaction of the court that his means are insufficient to enable him to pay for legal aid himself. This is a discretionary matter for each court and is currently not governed by any financial eligibility guidelines. In Finland, as a general principle, legal aid is granted in all criminal cases (except for simple criminal acts sanctioned with a fine). However, according to the Finnish respondent there exists a means test so it is not clear how this relates to the fact that – in principle – legal assistance free of charge is granted in all criminal cases. With regard to the existence of rules on how the suspect should prove that he is unable to pay for legal assistance, it should be noted that in more than half of the countries using a means test there are standardised application forms. This also means that in a considerable number of Member States (8) there is a means test without the existence of such standardised forms. In 11 countries there are rules on what documentation should be provided. In 5 countries there are (only or also) other rules than on what documentation should be provided (diagram 38). For example, in the Netherlands an income and property check is done through information available at the tax authorities. With regard to the existence of other legal criteria which the suspect has to meet to qualify for legal assistance (partially) free of charge 5 respondents answered that such criteria do exist. For example, in Cyprus the gravity, difficulty or other circumstances of the case are relevant. However, it should be noted that when specifying these 'other criteria', most of the remaining respondents refer to the general criteria for mandatory defence.

---

[96] A means test is a mechanism providing for uniform financial criteria which is used to evaluate whether the person applying for legal assistance free of charge is unable to cover (all or part of) the defence costs.

Diagram 37. Is there a means test to determine if the suspect is eligible for legal aid?

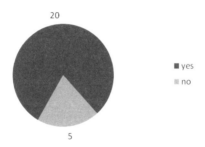

No means test: BG; DK; EE; LV; SE
Yes: AT; BE; CY; CZ; FI; FR; EL; HU; IE; IT; LT; LU; NL; PL; PT; RO; SK; SI; ES; UK

Diagram 38. If there is a means test, are there any rules on how the suspect should prove that he is unable to pay for legal assistance himself? More specifically are there:

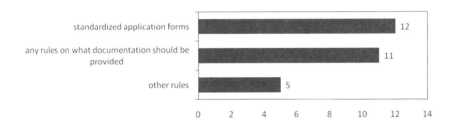

Standardized application forms: AT; BE; CY; FI; FR; EL; HU; LT; LU; NL; PT; SI
Any rules on what documentation should be provided: BE; CY; CZ; FI; HU; IT; LT; PT; RO; SK; ES
Other rules: AT; IE; NL; PL; UK

3.2.2   Procedure

In 4 Member States there is no legal obligation to inform the suspect of his right to legal assistance (partially) free of charge.[97] In the 21 Member States where such a legal obligation does exist, the moment at which the duty to inform the suspect of this right arises, varies: in about half of the countries the suspect should be informed immediately after arrest while in the other half the obligation arises at a given stage of the investigation or the proceedings. It should be mentioned however, that some of the respondents belonging to the second category – such as Cyprus and Poland – specify the given stage of the investigation or the proceedings (inter alia) as 'at the time of arrest'. So, it is fair to assume that they actually belong to the first category (countries where the obligation arises immediately after arrest). For the other countries belonging to the second category there is a considerable variation as to the contents of 'a given stage of the investigation or the proceedings'. It varies from within 6 hours after arrest (the Netherlands) to the moment the suspect appears before the examining judge in view of the trial (Greece). Only in France, does the obligation to inform the suspect of his right to legal assistance (partially) free of charge arise within a certain lapse of time after arrest, more specifically, when the suspect appears before the investigating judge (diagram 41).

In only 4 of the 21 countries where a legal obligation to inform the suspect exists, this information is provided to the suspect by means of a letter of rights.[98] In the majority of countries the suspect is informed orally (in 7 countries both orally and in writing). In Latvia and the Netherlands the suspect is only informed of his right to legal assistance (partially) free of charge in writing (diagram 42).

---

[97] BE; DK; LU: SE.
[98] AT; CZ; PL; SE.

Diagram 41. When does the duty to inform the suspect of his right to legal assistance (partially) free of charge arise?

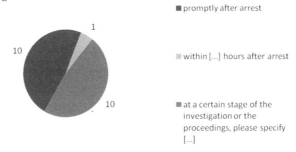

Promptly after arrest: BG; EE; FI; HU; IT; LV; PT; SK; ES; UK;

Within […] hours after arrest: FR

At a given stage of the investigation or the proceedings: AT; CY; CZ; EL; IE; LT; NL; PL; RO; SE

Diagram 42. How should the suspect be informed of his right to legal assistance (partially) free of charge?

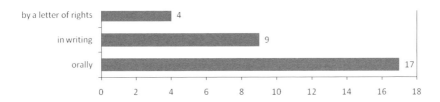

Letter of rights: AT; CZ; PL; SE

In writing: BG; EE; FI; FR; HU; LV; LT; NL; PT

Orally: AT; BG; CY; EE; FI; FR; EL; HU; IE; IT; LT; PT; RO; SK; ES; SE; UK

In the vast majority of the 21 Member States there is also an obligation to provide the information on the right to legal assistance (partially) free of charge in a language the suspect understands. Only in the Netherlands and Italy such an obligation does not exist.

There is a substantial divergence between Member States with regard to who decides on the request for free legal assistance (police, prosecutor, judge, legal aid board and/or other authority, see diagram 44). In 15 Member States only one authority is authorised to decide on legal assistance (partially) free of charge. In 9 of these countries it is only the judge who decides on a request for legal aid.[99] In 2 Member States (Spain and Belgium) this decision is exclusively taken by a legal aid board. In the other 4 countries the decision is left to an 'other authority'.[100] In almost all of the remaining 10 countries where more than one authority has the power to decide on legal aid, one of these authorities is the judge. Only in the UK the judge has no power in this respect – the decision is taken by the Scottish legal aid board and the Legal Services Commission in England and Wales.[101]

In about half of the 25 Member States offering suspects the possibility to apply for legal assistance (partially) free of charge there is a legal time limit for deciding on such requests. From the specifications of these legal time limits it is clear that some of them are rather vague: for example in the Czech Republic and Sweden the decision should be taken 'without delay'. More specific time limits vary widely from 48 hours (UK) to 6 weeks (the Netherlands). In a considerable number of countries (13) a legal time limit does not exist (diagram 45).

---

[99] However, the number is actually ten since Poland specified the 'other authority' as 'the president of the court or a judge authorized by him': both authorities being judges.
[100] These 'other authorities' are: a State Legal Aid Office (Finland), the President of the Bar Association (Luxembourg), the head of Social Security Services (Portugal) and a Legal Aid Authority forming part of the district court (Slovenia).
[101] However, this is different for Scotland where the judge does (also) have the power to decide on requests for free legal assistance.

Diagram 44. Who decides on the request for legal assistance (partially) free of charge?

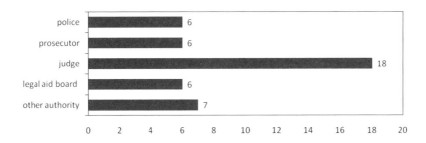

Police: BG; EE; FR; LV; LT; RO
Prosecutor: BG; EE; HU; LV; LT; RO
Judge: AT; BG; CY; CZ; DK; EE; FR; EL; HU; IE; IT; LV; LT; NL; PL; RO; SK; SE
Legal aid board: BE; FR; LT; NL; ES; UK
Other authority: BG; FI; LU; PL; PT; SI; UK

Diagram 45. Is there a legal time limit for deciding on the request for legal assistance (partially) free of charge?

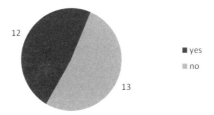

No legal time limit: AT; BG; CY; DK; EE; FI; EL; HU; IE; LV; LU; PL; RO
Yes: BE; CZ; FR; IT; LT; NL; PT; SK; SI; ES; SE; UK

In the majority of Member States (19) a legal remedy is available when the request for free legal assistance is denied. The contents of legal remedy vary from appeal according to criminal procedure law to administrative appeal. In Belgium the appeal should be filed with the labour court (tribunal de travail). In 6 Member States a legal remedy does not exist.

With regard to the factors that are taken into account when appointing a lawyer to provide legal assistance free of charge a small majority of the Member States (15) takes notice of the preference of the suspect. Only in 6 countries the specialisation of the lawyer is a relevant factor. The availability of the lawyer is taken into account in 11 countries (diagram 47). In 8 Member States only 'other factors' are considered when deciding on the appointment of a legal aid lawyer. In most cases, these 'other factors' concern the fact that the lawyer should be registered on a list of lawyers who declared to be willing to provide legal assistance free of charge.

When a request is granted, the decision on which lawyer should be appointed is taken by different authorities throughout the EU (diagram 48). In 3 countries[102] the judge is the sole authority to take such a decision whereas in 7 Member States the appointment of a specific lawyer is done only by the lawyer's professional organisation (bar). In 3 Member States[103] this decision can only be taken by the Legal Aid Board

Finally, 5 respondents declare that only an 'other authority' is empowered to decide which lawyer should be appointed. It should be mentioned however, that from the specifications provided by these respondents it turns out that in at least 3 cases the 'other authorities' are actually the judge (Poland) or the lawyer's professional organisation (Austria and Luxembourg) and therefore belong to the other categories mentioned before. Only in the UK the suspect himself is entitled to decide on which lawyer should be appointed, provided that the lawyer has a contract with the Legal Services Commission or the Scottish Legal Aid Board.

---

[102] EL; IE; SE.
[103] BE; LT; NL.

Diagram 47. When a request for legal assistance (partially) free of charge is approved, what factors are taken into account to decide which lawyer should be appointed?

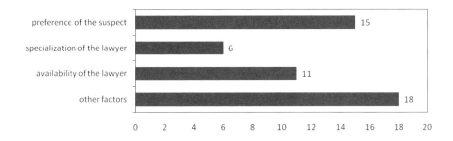

Preference of the suspect: BE; BG; CZ; DK; FI; FR; IT; LV; LT; LU; NL; PL; PT; SI; UK
Specialization of the lawyer: BE; BG; DK; LT; PL; RO
Availability of the lawyer: BE; BG; DK; EL; HU; LT; NL; PL; PT; RO; SI
Other factors: AT; BE; BG; CY; CZ; DK; EE; FI; FR; EL; IE; IT; LV; LT; SK; ES; SE; UK

Diagram 48. When a request for legal assistance (partially) free of charge is approved, who decides which lawyer should be appointed?

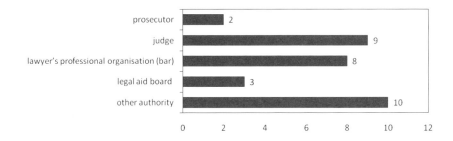

Prosecutor: EE; HU
Judge: CY; CZ; EE; FI; DK; EL; HU; IE; SE
Lawyer's professional organisation (bar): BG; EE; FR; LV; PT; RO; SK; ES
legal aid board: BE; LT; NL
other authority: AT; CY; CZ; FI; HU; IT; LU; PL; SI; UK

3.2.3   *Financial matters*

In almost all 25 Member States providing for legal assistance (partially) free of charge the costs of the defence lawyer are remunerated by the state. The only country where this is not the case is Hungary. Since this matter was not covered by the questionnaire, it is not clear who pays for the costs of legal assistance (partially) free of charge in Hungary.

The way in which remuneration by the state is provided, varies widely among the 24 Member States (diagram 50). In 6 countries the remuneration is provided per case. In 3 Member States the remuneration is awarded per hour and in only one country (Bulgaria) this happens per phase of the proceedings. In the remaining 14 Member States the remuneration is provided 'in another way'. From the specifications provided by the respondents it is clear that there are many different 'other ways' in which remuneration is awarded. For example, in Austria one lump sum is provided every year to the Bar by the Ministry of Justice as a compensation for providing legal assistance free of charge in civil and criminal matters. How this lump sum is used by the Bar and how the lawyers providing legal assistance free benefit of it is not explained by the Austrian respondent. While in most countries fixed fees are set by the government, in Estonia this is done by the Bar Association on a yearly basis. In Lithuania certain defence lawyers who provide legal assistance free of charge in criminal case on a regular basis (and who have entered into the relevant agreements with the service providing legal aid) are paid a regular monthly salary.[104]

---

[104] Defence lawyers who do not provide this kind of assistance on a regular basis, are paid a fixed fee for each case depending on the difficulty of the case.

Diagram 50. How is remuneration by the state of legal assistance (partially) free of charge provided?

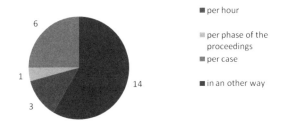

Per hour: FI; LU; RO

Per phase of het proceedings: BG

Per case: BE; FR; EL; PL; PT; SI

In another way: AT; CY; CZ; DK; EE; IE; IT; LV; LT; NL; SK; ES; SE; UK

In the majority of Member States remuneration for providing legal assistance free of charge is determined by minimum and/or maximum amount (diagram 51). The specifications of these minimum and/or maximum amounts are either not provided by the respondents, unclear or formulated in national currencies, which makes it difficult to compare this part of the information.

In half of the Member States providing for legal assistance (partially) free of charge, the suspect is obliged to pay a financial contribution (diagram 52). In a few countries, such as Austria, Estonia and Sweden, this is only possible in case of conviction and the financial situation of the convict is taken into account when deciding on the reimbursement of costs. In some other Member States (such as Belgium and the Slovak Republic) reimbursement is only possible when the suspect benefits from legal assistance partially free of charge (or 'for a reduced fee'). Spain takes a special position in this respect: according to Spanish 'free legal assistance law' the person who is entitled to free legal aid and who is sentenced to pay the costs of the trial, will only be obliged to pay the costs of his defence if his economic situation improves in the next 3 years.

Finally, the respondents were asked to provide numbers on the national budget for legal assistance (partially) free of charge in criminal proceedings and on this national budget as a percentage of the total criminal justice budget (See the diagram on the following page).

It is clear from these figures that there are huge differences among Member States with regard to the amount of money spent on legal assistance (partially) free of charge. However, it should be taken into account that 9 countries could not provide information on the national budget for legal assistance (partially) free of charge and that 3 Member States[105] could only provide for the total legal aid budget (without specifications for legal assistance free of charge in criminal cases). By far the largest criminal legal aid budget can be found in the UK (518.647.945 euro's, 25% of the total criminal justice budget). The smallest budget belongs to Cyprus (232.300 euro's, no data available on the percentage of the total criminal justice budget).

---

[105] IT; AT; PT.

Diagram 51. Are there any minimum and/or maximum amounts for remuneration for legal assistance (partially) free of charge?

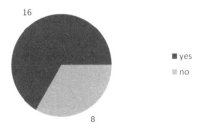

No minimum and/or maximum amounts: AT; BE; DK; EE; IT; LU; ES; SE

Yes: BG; CY; CZ; FI; FR; EL; IE; LV; LT; NL; PL; PT; RO; SK; SI; UK

Diagram 52. Is the suspect who benefits from legal assistance (partially) free of charge obliged to pay a financial contribution?

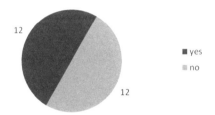

No obligation to pay financial contribution: BG; CY; CZ; DK; EL; IE; IT; LV; LU; PL; RO; SI

Yes: AT; BE; EE; FI; FR; LT; NL; PT; SK; ES; SE; UK

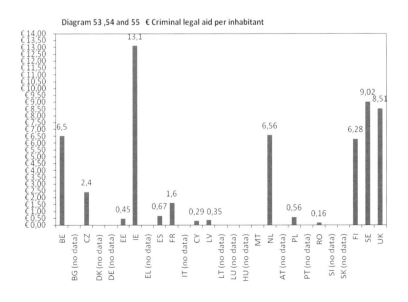

Diagram 53 ,54 and 55 € Criminal legal aid per inhabitant

Taking into account the total population of the different Member States, the amount of money available for criminal legal aid per inhabitant can be established. These numbers show the enormous differences between Member States when it comes to the amount of money available for legal assistance (partially) free of charge. As is shown from the picture below the 3 highest amounts per inhabitants are available in Ireland (13,1 euro's), Sweden (9,02 euro's) and the UK (8,51 euro's). In 6 – predominantly Central and Eastern European – countries this number of criminal legal aid per inhabitant is below one euro: Romania (0,16 euro's), Cyprus (0,29 euro's), Latvia (0,35 euro's), Estonia (0,45 euro's), Poland (0,56 euro's) and Spain (0,67 euro's).

	Criminal legal aid	Total budget legal aid	% criminal justice budget	Population million	€ criminal legal aid per inhabitant
	Euro's				
BE	54.220.000		6,4 %	8,3	6,5
BG	no data			10,6	
CZ	21.618.962		4,5%	7,6	2,4
DK	40.030.000		no data		
DE	no data			-	
EE	3.447.019		no data	1,3	0,45
IE	55.300.000		2,1%	4,2	13,1
EL	no data			11	
ES	30.900.000		1,61%	46,1	0,67
FR	103.000.000		no data	64,3	1,6
IT		86.562.704	no data	59	
CY	232.300		no data	0,8	0,29
LV	783.013		no data	2,2	0,35
LT	no data		no data	3,3	
LU	no data			0,5	
HU	no data			10	
MT					
NL	108.400.000		3,68%	16,5	6,56
AT		18.897.166	1,69 %	8,3	
PL	21.454.645		1,89 %	38	0,56
PT		42.306.500	no data	10,6	
RO	3.441.655		0,81%	21,5	0,16
SI	no data			2	
SK	no data			5,5	
FI	33.300.000		no data	5,3	6,28
SE	83.074.374		no data	9,2	9.02
UK	518.647.945		25%	60,9	8,51

3.2.4   Quality control

In the majority of Member States, providing legal assistance (partially) free of charge requires special qualifications. In 9 countries special qualifications are not required (diagram 56). It should be mentioned that in the specifications of these 'special qualifications' for providing legal assistance (partially) free of charge nearly half of the respondents refer to general requirements applying to all lawyers (such as being a member of the bar or having a lawyer's diploma) and not to any specific criteria that lawyers have to meet to be able to provide legal aid. In some Member States, such as Belgium, Bulgaria and Cyprus, the lawyer has to be registered on a list of lawyers who are willing to provide legal assistance free of charge. In Sweden the requirement for providing legal assistance free of charge is rather vague: only a lawyer, who is considered 'suitable for the assignment' shall be appointed as public defence counsel.[106] In Lithuania legal assistance free of charge may only be provided by defence lawyers who have entered into the relevant agreements with the services of legal assistance guaranteed by the state. In the Netherlands the lawyer who wants to provide legal assistance free of charge should prove to have finalised his law studies, to have practical experience in dealing with criminal cases and is obliged to participate in additional training every 2 years. He also has to meet certain requirements with regard to the organisation of his office.

More specific requirements can also be found in Spain where – according to an order of 1997 on the establishing of minimum general training and specialization requirements to provide free legal assistance services – the lawyer should have his usual residence and an open law firm in the Bar Association territory, 3 years of actual practicing and the Legal Practice School certificate.

---

[106] For special reasons, another suitable person whose qualifications make him eligible for appointment as a judge may be appointed as public defence counsel. The court should seek to engage advocates who regularly function as attorneys before the court.

Diagram 56. Are there any special qualifications for providing legal assistance (partially) free of charge?

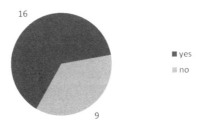

No special qualifications: AT; CZ; DK; EL; HU; IE; LV; LU; SI
Yes: BE; BG; CY; EE; FI; FR; IT; LT; NL; PL; PT; RO; SK; ES; SE; UK

Very sophisticated regulations exist in England and Wales where an important role is allocated to the Law Society in England and Wales (LSC). The LSC sets a number of requirements for solicitors' firms wishing to undertake criminal legal aid work under contract to the Legal Services Commission. Firms must hold the LSC's Specialist Quality Mark which focuses on the firm's management processes including file management, supervisory arrangements and training. All firms must have at least one supervisor who holds a specified minimum level of legal and managerial competence to supervise other caseworkers. Duty Solicitors wishing to undertake duty solicitor work at the police station and magistrates' court must hold a Duty Solicitor Qualification awarded by the Solicitors Regulation Authority. The LSC has also developed an independent peer review process involving a review of a random sample of files and which focuses on the quality of advice. This is gradually being rolled out across England and Wales. LSC contracts also specify certain performance standards which firms are required to meet and which are monitored by the LSC on an ongoing basis throughout the life of the contract.

In the majority of the other Member States (17) there are certain mechanisms to control the quality of legal assistance (partially) free of charge. In 8 countries though such control mechanisms do not exist (diagram 57). In most jurisdictions the supervision is carried out by the bar (diagram 58). In some Member States quality control is (inter alia) carried out by the government/the legal aid board.[107] In 6 countries 'other methods of quality control' exist. These concern mostly supervision by the judiciary (the judge having the power to withdraw an appointment and to appoint a new lawyer if the lawyer originally appointed does not function well). In Finland the performance of public legal aid attorneys and advocates is supervised by the Bar Association, the Chancellor of Justice as well as the court. In the E&W lawyers working under contract with the Legal Services Commission are thoroughly supervised by this commission.

---

[107] The Netherlands being the only country where this is the only form of control.

Diagram 57. Are there any mechanisms to control the quality of legal assistance (partially) free of charge?

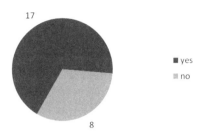

No control mechanisms: CY; EE; EL; HU; IE; LV; LU; SK
Yes: AT; BE; BG; CZ; DK; FI; FR; IT; LT; NL; PL; PT; RO; SI; ES; SE; UK

Diagram 58. What kinds of mechanisms exist to control the quality of legal assistance (partially) free of charge?

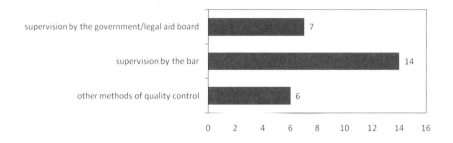

Supervision by the government/Legal aid board: BG; LT; NL; DK; ES; SE; UK
Supervision by the bar: AT; BE; BG; CZ; FI; DK; IT; LT; PL; PT; RO; ES; SE; UK
Other methods of quality control: FI; FR; PL; RO; SI; UK

3.2.5   *Legal assistance (partially) free of charge in special circumstances*

In the vast majority of Member States there are circumstances in which legal assistance in criminal proceedings is obligatory. Only in Ireland and the Netherlands there are no cases of obligatory defence.

As can be seen from diagram 60 there are many different grounds for mandatory legal assistance. In a considerable number of countries certain personal circumstances connected to the (physical or mental) condition of the suspect are relevant criteria (age, mental capacity or physical handicap of the suspect). The factual and/or legal complexity of the case is a relevant factor in only a small number of countries. However, the severity of the sanction that can be imposed is a ground for mandatory defence in a large number of Member States. The fact that the suspect is deprived of his liberty is a ground for obligatory defence in the majority of Member States (17).

In 19 countries there are also 'other circumstances' in which the assistance of a defence lawyer is obligatory. From the specifications provided for by the respondents it is clear that there are many different categories of such 'other circumstances'. However, certain grounds for mandatory defence appear in several Member States. Such as the fact that:

- the case is dealt with by a jury and/or by lay judges,
- the accused has no command of the language used in court,
- the case is tried in the absence of the accused,
- assistance by a defence lawyer is deemed necessary by the court,
- certain special (for example expedited or extradition) proceedings are followed or
- there is a conflict of defence interests between different suspects/accused and at least one of them already has a defence lawyer.

In Sweden obligatory defence does exist but without any particular grounds specified by law. Finally, it is worth mentioning that in Italy the assistance of a lawyer in criminal cases is always obligatory.

The costs for obligatory defence are covered by the state in almost all Member States. Only in Germany this is not the case.[108]

---

[108] It should be taken into account that 2 countries – the Netherlands and Ireland – did not answer this question.

Diagram 60. Which circumstances are grounds for obligatory defence?

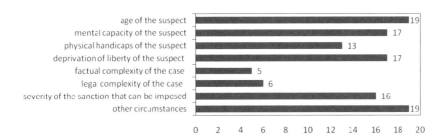

Age of the suspect: AT; BE; BG; CZ; EE; FI; FR; DE; EL; HU; LV; LT; LU; PL; PT; RO; SK; SI; UK

Mental capacity of the suspect: AT; BE; BG; CZ; EE; FI; FR; DE; EL; HU; LV; LT; PL; PT; SK; SI; UK

Physical handicaps of the suspect: AT; BG; CZ; EE; DE; HU; LV; LT; PL; PT; SK; SI; UK

Deprivation of liberty of the suspect: AT; BG; CZ; DK; EE; FI; FR; DE; HU; LT; NL; PL; PT; RO; SK; SI; UK

Factual complexity of the case: AT; BG; DE; EL; PL

Legal complexity of the case: AT; BG; DE; EL; PL; RO

Severity of the sanction that can be imposed: AT; BE; BG; CZ; DK; EE; FI; FR; DE; EL; HU; LT; PL; RO; SK; SI

Other circumstances: AT; BG; CY; CZ; DK; EE; FI; DE; HU; IT; LV; LT; PT; RO; SK; SI; ES; SE; UK

In the majority of countries the state always pays for the costs of obligatory defence, in a number of countries (9) this only happens sometimes (diagram 61). In Member States where the state 'sometimes' pays for mandatory defence 2 main categories of situations may be distinguished. Firstly, the situation in which mandatory legal assistance is only paid for by the state if the suspect is indigent and therefore qualifies for legal assistance (partially) free of charge. Secondly, there is the situation in which mandatory defence is – initially – paid for by the state. In case the accused is found guilty he can be obliged to reimburse the defence costs, although the financial situation of the convict will in most cases be taken in to account. Special reference should be made to Lithuania where – regardless of his entitlement to legal assistance guaranteed by the state – a suspect himself may enter into agreement on the provision of legal services with a private practicing defence lawyer. In this case, the costs must be covered by the suspect himself. Legal assistance guaranteed by the state can only be provided by defence lawyers who have entered into the relevant agreements with the services of legal assistance guaranteed by the state, and other attorneys or other 'special' lawyers may not be appointed. Therefore, in Lithuania, whether the costs for mandatory defence will be covered by the state will depend entirely on which defence lawyer has appeared in the case.

In the majority of Member States there is no possibility to appoint some sort of independent counsel such as amicus curiae or a special advocate. 8 countries[109] indicate that such a possibility does exist (diagram 62). However, from the specifications provided by these 8 countries it is clear that actual independent counsel as meant in the questionnaire only exists in some of these Member States.[110] For example, in Cyprus the Attorney General of the Republic can be appointed as amicus curiae when the interests of justice so require. Also, in England and Wales the ability to appoint special counsel covers such areas as public interest immunity hearings. There is a possibility to appoint "amicus curiae" in litigation before the Scottish courts, who do not appear as a party to a case/on direct instructions from a party, but who can e.g. offer information on a point of law or some other aspect of the case to assist the court in deciding a matter before it. However, in practice, it is not thought that much, if any, use is made of this possibility in criminal proceedings in Scotland.

---

[109] AT; BE; CY; DK; FR; LT; PL; UK.

[110] Some of the respondents refer to general mandatory defence counsel appointed by the court (Austria) or to representatives of social organisations (for example for the protection of human rights and freedoms) who may participate in the judicial proceedings if there is a need to protect the public interest represented by the organisation (Poland).

Diagram 61. Are the costs for obligatory defence covered by the state?

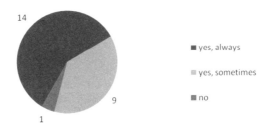

Costs sometimes covered by the state: BE; CZ; DK; EE; FR; HU; PL; PT; ES
Costs never covered by the state: DE
Costs always covered by the state: AT; BG; CY; FI; EL; IT; LV; LT; LU; RO; SK; SI; SE; UK

Diagram 62. Is there a possibility to appoint an independent counsel, such as an amicus curiae or special advocate?

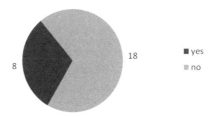

Possibility to appoint independent counsel: AT; BE; CY; DK; FR; LT; PL; UK
No: BG; CZ; EE; FI; DE; EL; HU; IE; IT; LV; LU; NL; PT; RO; SK; SI; ES; SE

3.2.6   Conclusions on the right to legal assistance (partially) free of charge

Although the right to legal assistance (partially) free of charge exists in all Member States (with the exception of one) there are considerable differences in the implementation of this right.

First of all, there is a wide variety in the way the eligibility for legal aid is to be determined: most Member States provide for some sort of merits and/or means test but the meaning and contents of these tests vary widely. In some countries the means test is very vague raising the question of its added value.

A second striking fact is that in 4 countries there is no legal obligation to inform the suspect of his right to legal assistance (partially) free of charge. Where this obligation does exist, there is considerable variation as to:

- the moment at which the obligation arises;
- the manner in which the information should be provided (only in a few countries the right to legal assistance free of charge is mentioned in a letter of rights);
- the authority deciding on the request for legal assistance (partially) free of charge and
- the authority deciding on which lawyer should be appointed.

The study also shows that in many countries there is no time limit for deciding on a request for legal aid; where such a time limit does exist it is often vague. In a few Member States there is no legal remedy available when the request for legal aid is denied. Also important is the fact that in the majority of countries the specialisation and the availability of the lawyer are not taken into account when deciding on which lawyer to appoint to a case.

Furthermore, there is a wide variety in the way in which legal assistance free of charge is remunerated. The information on the available budget for criminal legal aid provided by the Member States shows the enormous differences in financial recourses available for legal assistance free of charge. Especially in some Central and Eastern European countries the number of available criminal legal aid per habitant is remarkably low (below one euro). Also, striking is the fact that in a considerable number of countries such data are not available. This raises the question how the functioning of the legal aid system can be monitored and evaluated if such basic information on financial recourses is not known.

Although in most Member States there are special requirements for the lawyer providing legal assistance free of charge, in many cases it is clear from the specifications that these requirements are of a rather general nature and not limited to providing legal assistance free of charge. In a considerable number of countries there are no mechanisms to control the quality of legal assistance free of charge and – in other Member States – the authorities carrying out this kind of control vary widely. Consequently, there seems to be a substantial divergence in the way the quality of free legal assistance is controlled and ensured.

3.3 The right to translation of documents and the right to interpretation

3.3.1 The right to translation

In 5 Member States suspects do not have the right to be provided with a written translation of certain documents when he does not understand the language in which they are drawn up (diagram 63).

Procedure

Only 5 Member States have an established procedure for ascertaining whether there is a need for translation (diagram 64).[111]

In these Member States it will usually be the judge who decides whether translation is necessary. In the United Kingdom however, at early stages of proceedings, the police/prosecution will decide (while during court proceedings the court itself may also request translations).

In all Member States, translation of documents in criminal proceedings is provided at the state's expense.

In 9 Member States there are standard fees for legal translation of documents.

---

[111] Established procedure: BE; SK; EE

Diagram 63. When the suspect does not understand the language in which certain documents are drawn up, does he have the right to be provided with a written translation?

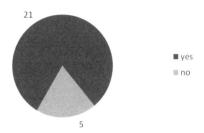

21

5

■ yes
■ no

No translation of documents: AT; BG; FR; LV; PT

Yes: BE; CY; CZ; DK; EE; FI; DE; EL; HU; IE; IT; LT; LU; NL; PL; RO; SK; SI; ES; SE; UK

Diagram 64. Is there an established procedure for ascertaining whether there is a need for translation of documents in criminal proceedings?

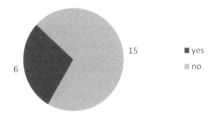

15

6

■ yes
■ no

No established procedure: CY; CZ; EE; FI; DE; EL; HU; IE; IT; LT; LU; NL; PL; RO; SI

Yes: BE; DK; SK; ES; SE; UK

Scope of the right to translation

In 21 Member States where there is a right to translation of documents, there is a considerable variation as to what extent this right applies to certain documents (diagram 68).

The majority of these Member States provides for a translation of the charge and the indictment.

Approximately half of these Member States provides for a translation of the detention order, the reasons for detention, the final judgment or 'other documents'.

Only a small number of these Member States provides for a translation of parts of the case file and the letter of rights.

Information on the right to translation

In 8 Member States there is no legal obligation to inform the suspect on his right to translation (diagram 69).

In only 4 of those Member States where such an obligation does exist, the duty to inform the suspect of the right to translation arises promptly after arrest. In the other Member States this duty arises at a certain stage of the investigation or the proceedings.

The way in which suspects are informed of their right to translation varies significantly (diagram 71). In 10 Member States where there is an obligation to inform the suspect on his right to translation, the suspect should be informed orally. In 3 Member States this should be done in writing. Only in 2 Member States this should be done by means of a letter of rights.

In 11 of those Member States where there is a legal obligation to inform the suspect on his right to translation, providing the information on this right in a language the suspect understands is legally obliged.

The right to written translation of important documents in criminal proceedings that are important for a suspect in order to be able to exercise his rights and prepare his defence is not provided in all Member States.

Diagram 68. Does the suspect have the right to be provided with a written translation of...?

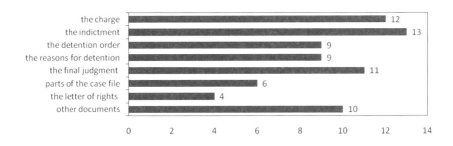

The charge: CZ; EE; DE; EL; HU; IE; IT; LT; LU; PL; SK; SI The indictment: CZ; EE; EL; HU; IE; IT; LT; LU; NL; PL; RO; SK; ES   The detention order: CZ; EL; HU; IT; LT; LU; PL; RO; SK The reasons for detention: CZ; EL; HU; IT; LT; LU; PL; RO; SK The final judgment: CZ; EE; FI; HU; IT; LT; LU; PL; RO; SK; ES Parts of the case file: EL; IT; LT; LU; RO; SK The letter of rights: LU; SK; ES; IT   Other: BE; CY; CZ; FI; DE; DK; HU; LT; SE; UK

Diagram 69. Is there a legal obligation to inform the suspect on his right to translation?

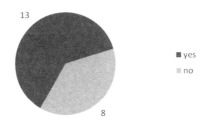

No legal obligation: DK; EE; FI; DE; IT; LU; NL; UK
Yes: BE; CY; CZ; EL; HU; IE; LT; PL; RO; SK; SI; ES; SE

Diagram 71. How should the suspect be informed of his right to translation?

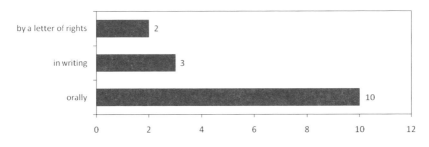

Orally: BE; CY; EL; HU; LT; RO; SK; SI; ES; SE;
In writing: HU; IE; LT
Letter of rights: CZ; PL

3.3.2 The right to interpretation

In all 26 Member States that responded, the suspect has the right to have the assistance of an interpreter when he does not understand the language used in the proceedings/in court.

Procedure

In 9 Member States there is an established procedure for ascertaining whether there is a need for interpretation in criminal proceedings (diagram 74). The majority of these Member States indicates that a judge will decide whether interpretation is necessary. 2 Member States, the Netherlands and the United Kingdom state that the police can decide autonomously whether the suspect is to be accorded the assistance of an interpreter. In nearly all Member States, interpretation is fully provided at the state's expense. Only in Austria this is done partly.

Member States greatly differ as to the presence of standard fees for legal interpretation. Only 14 Member States have standard fees. A similar division exists regarding the availability of a scheme for emergency linguistic assistance for suspects being held for questioning at the police station (12 Member States have such a scheme) and for emergency linguistic assistance in courts (11 Member States have such a scheme).

Scope of the right to interpretation

The extent to which the right to interpretation is guaranteed in Member States shows some variation (diagram 80). In all Member States that responded an interpreter will be present during the questioning of the suspect by the police or at trial when the suspect does not understand or speak the language of the proceedings. In 5 Member States an interpreter will not be present at the consultation of the suspect with his lawyer. The majority of Member States indicated that an interpreter will also be present at 'other procedural occasions/activities or hearings'. A remarkable finding is the difference between the availability of special provisions/arrangements for suspects who are visually or hearing impaired. Only half of the Member States have such special provisions for suspects who are visually impaired, while only 3 Member States[112] do not have special provision for suspects who are hearing impaired.

---

[112] EL; LV; SI.

Diagram 74. Is there an established procedure for ascertaining whether there is a need for interpretation in criminal proceedings?

Yes, established procedure: BE; DK; CY; NL; PT; SK; ES; SE; UK

No established procedure: AT; BG; CZ; EE; FI; FR; DE; EL; HU; IE; IT; LV; LT; LU; PL; RO; SI

Diagram 80. When the suspect does not understand the language used in the proceedings/in court, is an interpreter present at…?

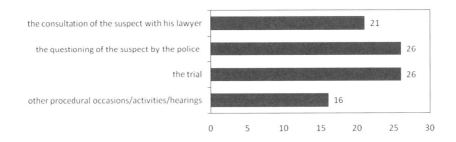

The consultation of the suspect with his lawyer: AT; CY; CZ; DK; EE; FI; DE; EL; IE; IT; LT; LU; NL; PL; PT; RO; SK; SI; ES; SE; UK

The questioning of the suspect by the police: AT; BE; BG; CY; CZ; DK; EE; FI; FR; DE; EL; HU; IE; IT; LV; LT; LU; NL; PL; PT; RO; SK; SI; ES; SE; UK

The trial: AT; BE; BG; CY; CZ; DK; EE; FI; FR; DE; EL; HU; IE; IT; LV; LT; LU; NL; PL; PT; RO; SK; SI; ES; SE; UK

Other procedural occasions/activities/hearings: BG; CY; CZ; DK; FR; DE; HU; IT; LV; LT; LU; NL; PL; PT; SE; UK

In 9 Member States there is no legal obligation to inform the suspect on his right to interpretation (diagram 83). In 8 of these 9 Member States the duty to inform the suspect of this right arises promptly after arrest. In the other Member States the duty arises at a certain stage of the investigation or the proceedings.

The way in which suspects are informed of their right to interpretation varies significantly (diagram 85). In 15 Member States, the suspect should be informed orally. In 3 Member States this should be done in writing. In 6 Member States this should be done by means of a letter of rights. Only one Member State (Luxembourg) that indicated that the suspect should be informed in writing also indicated the presence of a letter of rights.

In 15 of those Member States where there is a legal obligation to inform the suspect on his right to interpretation, providing the information on this right in a language the suspect understands is legally obliged.

3.3.3   *Conclusions on the right to translation and interpretation in criminal proceedings*

Although the right to interpretation exists in all Member States and the right to translation of documents is guaranteed in all but 5 Member States, the analysis shows a great divergence regarding the implementation of these rights. This divergence specifically applies to whether there is a legal obligation to be informed on these rights and to the scope of the rights.

Diagram 83. Is there a legal obligation to inform the suspect on his right to interpretation?

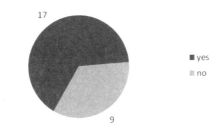

No legal obligation: BG; DK; EE; FI; FR; DE; IT; LU; NL
Yes: AT; BE; CY; CZ; EL; HU; IE; LV; LT; PL; PT; RO; SK; SI; ES; SE; UK

Diagram 85. How should the suspect be informed of his right to interpretation?

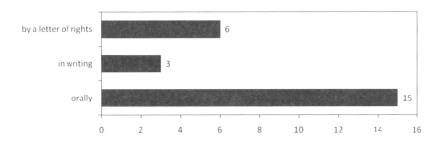

Orally: AT; BE; CY; EL; HU; IE; LV; LT; LU; PT; RO; SK; SI; ES; SE
In writing: HU; LI; LU
Letter of rights: AT; CZ; LU; PL; SE; UK

3.4 Other fundamental guarantees and the right to be informed on them

3.4.1 Information on the right to be informed on the charge

All Member States accord the suspect the right to be informed on the charge (nature and cause of the accusation against him). In 5 Member States however there is no legal obligation to inform the suspect on his right to be informed on the charge.

In nearly all Member States where there is a duty to inform the suspect on his right to be informed on the charge, this duty arises at a given stage of the investigation or the proceedings, even in situations without arrest. In one Member State (Belgium) this duty arises within [...] hours after arrest. In another Member State (Greece) this duty arises promptly after arrest.

The way in which suspects are informed of their right to be informed on the charge varies significantly (diagram 90). In 17 Member States, the suspect should be informed orally. In 9 Member States this should be done in writing. In 7 Member States this should be done by means of a letter of rights.

In 18 of those Member States where there is a legal obligation to inform the suspect on his right to be informed on the charge, providing the information on this right in a language the suspect understands is legally obliged.

Diagram 90. How should the suspect be informed of his right to be informed on the charge?

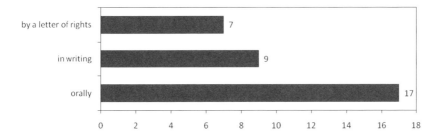

Orally: AT; BE; BG; CY; DK; EE; EL; HU; IE; IT; LT; LU; RO; SK; SI; SE; UK
In writing: BE; BG; EE; HU; LI; LU; PT; RO; UK
Letter of rights: AT; CZ; LV; LU; PL; SE; UK

3.4.2   Information on access to the file

The right for a suspect to have access to the file is not guaranteed throughout the EU. In 4 Member States, this right is not provided.[113] Moreover, in 6 of those Member States where such a right exists, there is no legal obligation to inform the suspect on his right to have access.[114] In 2 of those Member States providing the information on this right in a language the suspect understands is not legally obliged.

In nearly all Member States where there is a duty to inform the suspect on his right to have access to the file, this duty arises at a given stage of the investigation or the proceedings, even in situations without arrest. In 2 Member States (Greece and the Slovak Republic) this duty arises promptly after arrest. The way in which suspects are informed of their right to have access to the file varies significantly (diagram 95). In 12 Member States, the suspect should be informed orally. In 3 Member States this should be done in writing. In 5 Member States this should be done by means of a letter of rights.

 Finally, the great majority of Member States where the right to have access exists, provides the suspect with a written translation of the indictment, the detention order, the reasons for detention and the final judgment (diagram 97).

---

[113] EE; FR; DE; ES.
[114] BE; DK; FI; LU; NL; UK.

Diagram 95. How should the suspect be informed of the right to have access to the file?

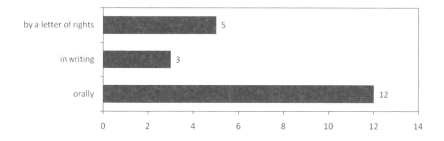

Orally: AT; BG; CY; EL; IE; IT; LT; PT; RO; SK; SI; SE
In writing: BG; HU; LT
Letter of rights: AT; CZ; IT; LV; PL

Diagram 97. Does the suspect have the right to be provided with a written version of...?

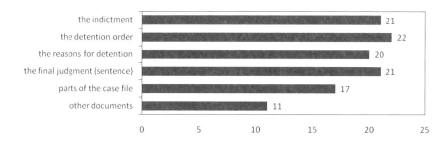

The indictment: BE; BG; CY; CZ; DK; EE; FI; FR; DE; EL; HU; IE; IT; LT; LU; NL; PL; PT; RO; SK; SI

The detention order: BE; BG; CY; CZ; DK; EE; FI; FR; DE; EL; HU; IE; IT; LV; LT; LU; NL; PL; PT; RO; SK; SI

The reasons for detention: BE; BG; CY; CZ; DK; EE; FI; FR; DE; EL; HU; IT; LT; LU; NL; PL; PT; RO; SI; ES

The final judgment (sentence): BE; BG; CY; CZ; DK; FI; FR; DE; EL; HU; IT; LV; LT; LU; NL; PL; PT; RO; SK; SI; ES

Parts of the case file: BE; BG; CY; DK; FI; DE; EL; IT; LV; LT; LU; NL; PL; PT; RO; SK; SI

Other documents: AT; CY; CZ; EE; DK; HU; LV; LT; SI; SE; UK

3.4.3   Information on the right to remain silent

The right for a suspect to remain silent during criminal investigations and proceedings is not provided for in 2 Member States (Luxembourg and France) (diagram 98). Moreover, in 2 of those Member States where such a right exists, there is no legal obligation to inform the suspect on his right to remain silent (Belgium and Finland). In one Member State (the Netherlands) providing the information on this right in a language the suspect understands is not legally obliged.

In nearly all Member States where there is a duty to inform the suspect on his right to remain silent, this duty arises at a given stage of the investigation or the proceedings. In 5 Member States this duty arises promptly after arrest.[115] In most Member States suspects should be informed orally on their right to remain silent. In 5 Member States this should be done in writing. In 4 Member States this should be done by means of a letter of rights (diagram 101).

---

[115] EL; IR; LV; SK; ES

Diagram 98. Does the suspect have a right to remain silent during criminal investigations and proceedings?

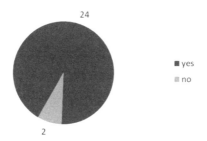

Yes: AT; BE; BG; CY; CZ; DK; EE; FI; DE; EL; HU; IE; IT; LV; LT; NL; PL; PT; RO; SK; SI; ES; SE; UK
No: FR; LU

Diagram 101. How should the suspect be informed of his right to remain silent?

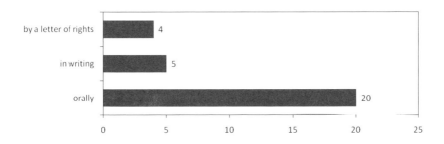

Orally: AT; BG; CY; DK; EE; DE; EL; HU; IE; IT; LV; LT; NL; PT; RO; SK; SI; ES; SE; UK.
In writing: BG; EE; LT; RO; UK.
Letter of rights: AT; CZ; PL; UK.
No right to remain silent: FR; LU

3.4.4 Information on the right to call and examine witnesses/experts

The right for a suspect to call and examine witnesses or experts is not provided for in 2 Member States (Latvia and Portugal). In 6 Member States where such a right exists, there is no legal obligation to inform the suspect on the right to call and examine witnesses.[116] In 2 Member States (the Netherlands and Ireland) providing the information on this right in a language the suspect understands is not legally obliged.

In 15 Member States where there is a duty to inform the suspect on his right to call and examine witnesses or experts, this duty arises at a given stage of the investigation or the proceedings. In 2 Member States (Slovak Republic and Spain) this duty arises promptly after arrest and in one Member State within [...] hours after arrest (the Netherlands). In the majority of Member States suspects should be informed orally on their right to call and examine witnesses or experts. In 6 Member States this should be done in writing. In 3 Member States this should be done by means of a letter of rights (diagram 106).

3.4.5 Conclusions on other fundamental guarantees and the right to be informed on them

A striking finding is the fact that fundamental rights such as the right to remain silent, to have access to the file and to call and/or examine witnesses or experts are not provided for in all Member States. A remark applicable to all the rights described above (including the right to be informed on the charge) is the substantial divergence in the way suspects are informed as well as the absence of a general legal obligation to be informed on these rights.

---

[116] BE; DK; FI; FR; EL; LU.

Diagram 106. How should the suspect be informed of his right to call and examine witnesses/experts?

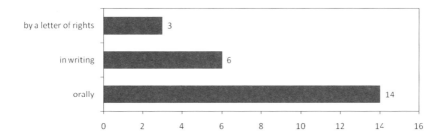

Orally: AT; BG; CY; EE; HU; IE; IT; LT; RO; SK; SI; ES; SE; UK
In writing: BG; EE; DE; LT; NL; SE
Letter of rights: AT; CZ; PL

3.5   European arrest warrant and other mutual recognition instruments

3.5.1   With respect to the European Arrest Warrant: are the same rights as mentioned in chapter 1-4 applicable to EAW proceedings?

The right to legal advice as guaranteed in domestic cases applies in all Member States with respect to the European Arrest Warrant (diagram 108).[117] With regard to the right to legal assistance free of charge, 2 Member States (Germany and Sweden) reported that this right is only partly applicable to EAW proceedings.

4 Member States only partly apply the right to interpretation and the right to translation of documents to EAW proceedings.[118]

Nearly all Member States apply the right to information concerning fundamental procedural rights equally to EAW proceedings. 2 Member States (France and United Kingdom) restrict this information to the right to be informed on the charge.

---

[117] 1 Member State (Sweden) indicated that this is only partly the case but the specifications of the questionnaire reveal that in fact the same right applies "as during an ordinary Swedish preliminary investigation and trial".
[118] FR; NL; SE; UK.

Diagram 108. Does the right to legal advice apply to proceedings concerning the European Arrest Warrant?

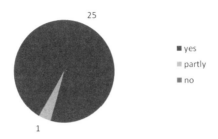

Partly: SE

Yes: AT; BE; BG; CY; CZ; DK; EE; FI; FR; DE; EL; HU; IE; IT; LV; LT; LU; NL; PL; PT; RO; SK; SI; ES; UK

No: -

3.5.2 With respect to the Framework Decision on the Application of the Principle of Mutual Recognition to Financial Penalties: are the same rights as mentioned in Chapter 1-4 applicable to these proceedings?

The right to legal advice as guaranteed in domestic cases does not apply in all Member States with respect to the Framework Decision on the Application of the Principle of Mutual Recognition to Financial Penalties (diagram 112). In 2 Member States (Germany and Slovenia) this right is not provided for. In 6 Member States the right to legal advice is only partly applied to these proceedings. With regard to the right to legal assistance free of charge, several Member States reported that this right is not (3)[119] or only partly (5)[120] applicable to such proceedings.

4 Member States only partly apply the right to interpretation and the right to translation of documents to these proceedings while in such cases 3 Member States do not provide for these rights at all.[121]

In 19 Member States the right to information concerning fundamental procedural rights is applied equally to these proceedings. One Member State (Slovak Republic) only provides for the right to information on the charge while one Member State (Austria) applies the right to information on access to the file, on the right to remain silent and on the right to call or examine witnesses/experts but not to information on the charge.

---

[119] DE; IR; SI.
[120] FR; IT; NL; SK; SE.
[121] FR; DE; SI.

Diagram 112. Does the right to legal advice apply to the Framework decision on the Application of the Principle of Mutual Recognition to Financial Penalties?

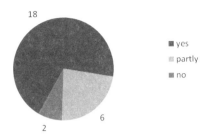

No: DE; SI

Partly: BG; IT; NL; SK; SE; UK

Yes: AT; BE; CY; CZ; DK; EE; FI; FR; EL; HU; IE; LV; LT; LU; PL; PT; RO; ES

3.5.3 With respect to the Framework Decision on the execution in the European Union of orders freezing property or evidence: are the same rights as mentioned in chapter 1-4 applicable to these proceedings?

The right to legal advice as guaranteed in domestic cases does not apply in all Member States with respect to the Framework Decision on the execution in the EU of orders freezing property or evidence (diagram 116). In 1 Member State (Slovenia) this right is not provided for. In 5 Member States the right to legal advice is only partly applied to these proceedings. With regard to the right to legal assistance free of charge, several Member States reported that this right is not (2)[122] or only partly (6)[123] applicable to such proceedings.

3 Member States only partly apply the right to interpretation and the right to translation of documents to these proceedings while in such cases 2 Member States (France and Slovenia) do not provide for these rights at all.

In 21 Member States the right to information concerning fundamental procedural rights is applied equally to these proceedings. One Member State (Austria) applies the right to information on the charge, on the access to the file, on the right to remain silent but not on the right to call or examine witnesses/experts.

3.5.4 With respect to the Framework Decision on the Application of the Principle of Mutual Recognition on Confiscation Orders are the same rights as mentioned in chapter 1-4 applicable to these proceedings?

The right to legal advice as guaranteed in domestic cases does not apply in all Member States with respect to the Framework Decision on the Application of the Principle of Mutual Recognition on Confiscation Orders (diagram 120). In 2 Member States this right is not provided for. In 6 Member States the right to legal advice is only partly applied to these proceedings. With regard to the right to legal assistance free of charge, several Member States reported that this right is not (4)[124] or only partly (4)[125] applicable to such proceedings.

---

[122] IR; SI.
[123] AT; FR; DE; IT; NL; SE.
[124] DE; IR; LI; SI.
[125] FR; IT; NL; SE.

Diagram 116. Does the right to legal advice apply to proceedings concerning the Framework Decision on the Execution in the EU of Orders Freezing Property or evidence?

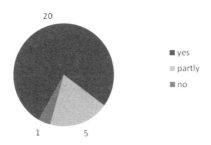

No: SI

Partly: AT; IT; NL; SE; UK

Yes: BE; BG; CY; CZ; DK; EE; FI; FR; DE; EL; HU; IE; LV; LT; LU; PL; PT; RO; SK; ES

Diagram 120. Does the right to legal advice apply to proceedings concerning the Framework Decision on the Application of the Principle of Mutual Recognition on Confiscation Orders?

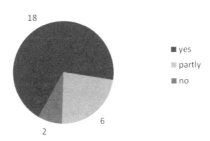

Yes: AT; BE; CY; CZ; DK; EE; FI; FR; EL; HU; IE; LV; LU; PL; PT; RO; SK; ES

Partly: BG; IT; LT; NL; SE; UK

No: DE; SI

3 Member States only partly apply the right to interpretation and the right to translation of documents to these proceedings while in such cases 4 Member States[126] do not provide for these rights at all.

In 19 Member States the right to information concerning fundamental procedural rights is applied equally to these proceedings. One Member State (Austria) applies the right to information on access to the file, on the right to remain silent and on the right to call or examine witnesses/experts but not on information on the charge.

3.5.5   *Conclusions on the European Arrest Warrant and other mutual recognition instruments*

When comparing the results of the analysis between the various mutual recognition instruments, some main findings can be distinguished quite easily. Firstly, the European Arrest Warrant (EAW) clearly is the instrument that is treated the most as being equal to the domestic proceedings. The right to legal advice, for example, is applied to EAW proceedings in all Member States in the same way as for domestic cases. Secondly, conclusions as to the 'partial' application of certain rights with regards to mutual recognition instruments should be made with caution since some Member States have responded in this way when the particular instrument has not yet been implemented into national law. Thirdly, those Member States not applying certain rights with regards to the various mutual recognition instruments are often the same. Finally, the great majority of Member States applies the right to information on fundamental procedural guarantees to the mutual recognition proceedings equally as for domestic proceedings.

---

[126] FR; DE; LI; SI.

4 Conclusions and analysis of conformity with ECHR standards

4.1 The right to information

In this study "the right to information" is dealt with as an overarching horizontal issue that is highly relevant for procedural rights being practical and effective. We have distinguished 2 dimensions. First, the right of anyone charged with a criminal offence to be informed on the nature and cause of the accusations against him and to have access to the evidence on which these accusations are based as guaranteed by Art. 5 and 6 ECHR). Secondly, the right to information in the sense of being informed on fundamental procedural rights, which as such is not covered by the ECHR.

A notable finding of this study is the fact that the right to remain silent is no statutory right in France and Luxembourg and the right to have access to the file is not provided for on behalf of the suspect in legislation in Estonia, France, Germany and Spain, both being basic requirements of a fair trial in the ECHR.

A remark applicable to all the rights that are the subject of this study (including the right to be informed on the charge) is the substantial divergence in the way suspects are informed as well as the absence of legal obligations for the authorities to inform the suspect on these fundamental procedural rights.

With regards to the right to contact a lawyer after arrest, all Member States have a legal obligation to inform the suspect on this right, but this information is not always given immediately after arrest. Also, the moment at which the obligation to inform the suspect of his right to have a lawyer present during police interrogation varies from promptly after arrest until a later stage in the investigation or proceedings. This right is obviously only effective when the suspect is timely informed on it and if he is offered the opportunity to contact a lawyer before the first police interrogation. In many Member States where there is a right to legal assistance during police interrogation, there are no provisions to secure the effectuation of this right.

The same applies to information on the right to legal aid. In 4 Member States there is no legal obligation to inform the suspect of the right to legal assistance (partially) free of charge and in the remainder of the Member States where a legal obligation to inform the suspect does exist, the moment at which the duty arises varies considerably as well as the manner in which the information is given. In the majority of the countries the information is given orally and in only 4 countries this information is provided in a letter of rights.

A similar picture can be drawn with regard to information on the right to interpretation and translation. In 8 Member States there is no legal obligation to inform the suspect on his right to interpretation and in 9 Member States there is no obligation to inform the suspect on his right to translation.

Striking is that in Belgium and Finland there is no legal obligation to inform the suspect of his right to remain silent and in 6 Member States there is no obligation to inform the suspect of his right to call and examine witnesses.

In 10 Member States the suspect is informed about (one or more of) his rights by means of a Letter of rights (Austria, Czech Republic, England and Wales, Italy, Latvia, Luxemburg, Poland, Slovak Republic , Spain and Sweden). However, there are great differences between these EU Member States as to which rights are included. Many Letters of Rights do not mention the right to remain silent or the right to translation or interpretation and sometimes there is no letter of rights available in the language the suspect understands.

4.2   The right to legal assistance

According to the case law of the ECtHR the right to contact a legal advisor – as part of the general right to legal assistance which is covered by Art. 6 § 3 b and c ECHR – arises immediately upon arrest. The study shows that the right to contact a lawyer after arrest exists in most Member States. However, there is a great divergence as to the moment at which the right to contact a lawyer can be effected. For example, in a considerable number of countries this is not possible immediately after arrest – as required by the ECHR – but only at a given stage of the investigation or the proceedings.

Also, it follows from recent judgments of the ECtHR that access to a lawyer should as a rule be provided as from the first interrogation of a suspect by the police, unless it is demonstrated in the light of the particular circumstances of the case that there are compelling reasons to restrict this right. Furthermore, the ECtHR has held that the lack of legal assistance during a suspect's interrogation would constitute a restriction of his defence rights and that these rights will in principle be irretrievably prejudiced when incriminating statements made during police interrogation without access to a lawyer are used for a conviction.

It can be concluded from the study that the basic rules mentioned above are not common practice throughout the EU: in 4 Member States the right to consult a lawyer before questioning is not guaranteed[127] and in 5 Member States there is

---

[127] In the Netherlands this has changed as a result of the Salduz judgment of the ECtHR Grand Chamber, 27 November 2008, *Salduz* (no. 36391/02). Requested to give an interpretation of the

no right for the lawyer to be present at interrogations carried out by the police. In almost all countries where the lawyer is allowed to be present, authorities are obliged to inform the suspect of this right but there are considerable differences among Member States as to the moment at which the obligation to inform the suspect of this right arises and the way in which the information is provided to the suspect. Furthermore, in several countries there is no possibility for the defence to deliberate in private during questioning. Finally, the study shows that the presence of a lawyer at the interrogation is not deemed indispensable: only in 3 Member States it is not allowed to use the confession of a suspect made in the absence of his lawyer as evidence in court.

4.3 The right to legal assistance (partially) free of charge

With respect to the right to legal assistance (partially) free of charge – as guaranteed by Art. 6 § 3 c ECHR – it follows from the case law of the ECtHR that Member States have a certain margin of appreciation in choosing a system that appears to them to be most effective. However, free legal assistance should always be available where the interests of justice demands it. The study shows that although the right to legal assistance (partially) free of charge exists in all Member States (with the exception of one) there are considerable differences in the implementation of this right. Especially striking is the wide variety in merits and/or means tests. Also important is the fact that in a small number of countries there is no legal obligation to inform the suspect of his right to legal assistance (partially) free of charge. Where this obligation does exist, there is considerable variation as to the scope of this obligation. Besides the differences in the applicable legal frameworks regulating the right to legal assistance free of charge, the study also shows enormous differences in financial recourses available for legal aid. The remarkable low budgets of some countries raise the question whether despite existing guarantees in the applicable legal framework, it is in – in everyday practice – in fact possible to effectuate the right to free legal assistance whenever the interest of justice demands it.

---

consequences of this judgment for the Dutch practice the Supreme Court of the Netherlands ruled on 30 June 2009 that a suspect has the right to consult a lawyer before the first police interrogation, but that only a juvenile suspect has the right to also have a lawyer present during police interrogation (HR 30 June 2009, no. 2411.08 J, NbSr 2009, 249.

4.4   Quality of legal assistance (partially) free of charge

The study allows making some remarks as to the quality of the legal assistance (partially) free of charge and the responsibilities of the State in this respect. Although it is clear from the case law of the ECtHR that the lawyer's conduct is essentially an affair between the lawyer and his client, the State is under the obligation to ensure that legal assistance is actually effective. As a result, the Member States need to foresee in some sort of monitoring system. The study shows that in a considerable number of countries there are no mechanisms to control the quality of legal assistance free of charge and – in other Member States – the authorities carrying out this kind of control vary widely. Consequently, there seems to be a substantial divergence in the way the quality of free legal assistance is controlled and ensured. Also, the 'special' requirements for the lawyer providing legal assistance free of charge are, in many cases, of a rather general nature and not limited to providing legal assistance free of charge. Moreover, in the majority of countries the specialisation and the availability of the lawyer are not taken into account when deciding on which lawyer to appoint to a case.

These findings raise the question whether the quality of legal assistance (partially) free of charge is in fact sufficiently guaranteed throughout the EU.

4.5   The right to interpretation and translation

Although the right to interpretation exists in all Member States, the right to translation of documents is guaranteed in all but 5 Member States. The analysis shows a great divergence regarding the implementation of these rights. This divergence specifically applies to the fact whether there is a legal obligation to be informed on these rights and to the scope of the rights. In 5 Member States there is no provision for interpretation at the consultation of the suspect with his lawyer and some Member States have no provisions for suspects who are visually impaired or hearing impaired. There is also a considerable variety in what documents have to be provided to the suspect, and what documents are translated. It appears from the study that only a slight majority of the Member States provides a written translation of the charge, the detention order, or the final judgment. A letter of rights is only translated in 4 of the 10 countries that provide for a letter of rights. The results of the study show that on the level of practical implementation of the right to interpretation and translation there is a divergence with the requirements that derive from the case law of the ECtHR as summarised in § 2.4.

4.6   Procedural rights in the mutual recognition instruments

When comparing the results of the analysis between the various mutual recognition instruments, some main findings can be distinguished quite easily. First, the European Arrest Warrant (EAW) clearly is the instrument that is treated the most as being equal to the domestic proceedings. The right to legal advice, for example, is applied to EAW proceedings in all Member States in the same way as for domestic cases. Secondly, conclusions as to the 'partial' application of certain rights with regards to mutual recognition instruments should be made with caution since some Member States have responded in this way when the particular instrument has not yet been implemented into national law. Thirdly, those Member States not applying certain rights with regards to the various mutual recognition instruments are often the same. Finally, the great majority of Member States applies the right to information on fundamental procedural guarantees to the mutual recognition proceedings equally as for domestic proceedings.

4.7   Conclusion

A striking finding is the fact that fundamental rights such as the right to remain silent, to have access to the file and to call and/or examine witnesses or experts, that are basic requirements of a fair trial in the ECHR are not provided for in legislations of all Member States.

In general, it follows from the study that although the 4 procedural rights that were subject of this research – the right to information, the right to legal advice, the right to legal assistance (partially) free of charge and the right to interpretation and translation – seem to be guaranteed by law more or less in accordance with the ECHR in the criminal justice systems of the EU. However a more in depth look at the implementation of these rights raises doubts as to whether in all Member States everyday practice is in line with the Strasbourg standard. This underlines the need for EU action.

5   List of Contacts

Country	Name	Surname	Email address
AT	Christian	Pilnacek	pilnacek@bmj.gv.at
AT	Bernhard	Weratschnig	bernhard.weratschnig@bmj.gv.at
BE	Charlotte	Janssens	charlotte.janssensdebisthoven@just.fgov.be
BG	Millen a	Stover	m_stoeva@justice.government.bg
CZ	Suzanne	Cernecka	zcernecka@msp.justice.cz
CY	Phedra	Gregoriou	pgregoriou@mjpo.gov.cy
DK	M. Niels	Jakobsen	mnj@jm.dk
EE	Markko	Künnapu	markko.kynnapu@just.ee
FI	Kirsi	Pulkinen	kirsi.m.pulkkinen@om.fi
FR	Eric	Ruelle	eric.ruelle@justice.gouv.fr
DE	Martina	Hornstein	hornstein-ma@bmj.bund.de
EL	Dimitris	Zimianitis	dzimiani@gmail.com
HU	Eszter	Viczko	viczkoe@irm.gov.hu
IE	Ger	Moore	gmmoore@justice.ie
IE	Billy	Keane	bjkeane@justice.ie
IT	Lorenzo	Salazar	lorenzo.salazar@giustizia.it
LV	Zigmunds	Dundurs	zigmund.dundurs@tm.gov.lv
LT	Jevgenijus	Kuzma	j.kuzma@tm.lt
LU	Sarah	Khabirpour	sarah.khabirpour@mj.etat.lu
MT	Josette	Zerafa	josette.zerafa@gov.mt
NL	Adrienne	Boerwinkel	a.boerwinkel@minjus.nl
PL	Alicja	Klamczyńska	klamczynska@ms.gov.pl
PL	Rafał	Kierzynka	kierzynka@ms.gov.pl
PT	Antonio	Delicado	antoniodelicado@dgpj.mj.pt
RO	Alina	Barbu	abarbu@just.ro
SK	Jana	Vnukova	jana.vnukova@justice.sk
SI	Matevz	Pezdirc	matevz.pezdirc@gov.si
ES	Almudena	Darias	almudena.darias@mjusticia.es
SE	Signe	Öhman	signe.ohman@justice.ministry.se
UK	Rosalind	Campion	rosalind.campion@homeoffice.gsi.gov.uk

6 List of Diagrams[128]

---

[128] This is a list of the diagrams used in the Report, numbered according to the number of the question in the questionnaire. For an overview of **all** diagrams of the questionnaire per question, see Annex 2